Slumach's Gold

Slumach's Gold
IN SEARCH OF A LEGEND

Rick Antonson, Mary Trainer
and Brian Antonson

VICTORIA • VANCOUVER • CALGARY

Heritage House Publishing
 Company Ltd.
#108 – 17665 66A Avenue
Surrey, BC V3S 2A7
www.heritagehouse.ca

Library and Archives Canada Cataloguing in Publication
Antonson, Rick, 1949-
   Slumach's gold: in search of a legend/Rick Antonson,
Mary Trainer, Brian Antonson.
Includes bibliographical references and index.

ISBN 978-1-894974-35-6

   1. Slumach, d. 1891. 2. Gold mines and mining—British Columbia—
Pitt Lake Region—History. 3. Abandoned gold mines—British
Columbia—Pitt Lake Region—History. 4. Pitt Lake Region (B.C.)—
History. 5. Gold miners—British Columbia—Biography. I. Trainer,
Mary, 1948- II. Antonson, Brian, 1948- III. Title.

FC3845.P57A58 2007   971.1'33   C2007-903906-5

Edited by Karla Decker
Proofread by Marial Shea
Book design by Frances Hunter
Cover design by Ruth Linka
Sketches by Fred Bosman
Map of Slumach country by Darlene Nickull
Printed in Canada

Heritage House acknowledges the financial support for its publishing program from the Government of Canada through the Book Publishing Industry Development Program (BPIDP), Canada Council for the Arts, and the province of British Columbia through the British Columbia Arts Council and the Book Publishing Tax Credit.

The Canada Council | Le Conseil des Arts
for the Arts | du Canada

BRITISH COLUMBIA
ARTS COUNCIL
We acknowledge the support of the Province of British Columbia
through the British Columbia Arts Council

Contents

Dedication

With admiration and deep appreciation, this
35th-anniversary edition is dedicated to N.L. (Bill) Barlee,
inspiring high-school history teacher, historian, author, raconteur,
entrepreneur, politician, television documentarian and museum
collector/curator. As editor and publisher of the magazine *Canada
West* between 1969 and 1982, Bill captured the hearts and minds of
many people (the authors of this book among them) as he brought
British Columbia's history to life. His *Gold Creeks and Ghost Towns*
(1971) is still an influential work decades later. He was an early writer
about (and believer in) Slumach's gold. Bill became a friend of *In
Search of A Legend* when we first published it in 1972, and
has remained so. Thank you, Bill, for your personal support
and for all you have done for our province.

Dedication to the 1972 edition

Hidden in every legend is the first person that ever told
the story. This work is dedicated to such folk. Were it not for
them, we would be without the parts of our history that
are the cornerstones of our heritage.

Prologue

The fisherman's elderly wife leaned her frail body over the campfire. The flame glowed into the dark where she sat on a log stump, lighting the wrinkles around her mouth. She let her words flow slowly into the night's circle of six young boys. "There's a lost gold mine up on Pitt Lake," she began. "But you'll never find it—'least not find it and live." Her gaze flickered from boy to boy until she'd locked stares with each pair of innocent eyes.

Two of us were brothers, and her story gripped our imagination in a particular way. When she spoke, we believed every word she said about a $100-million mystery—a mystery that would remain unsolved for more than a century.

The fire that night was on the shore of Hatzic Lake, near Mission, British Columbia, the site of our week-long boys' camp. It was summer 1957. The fisherman had been teaching us outdoor skills that day, everything from the fine art of stabbing worms onto an open hook so they wriggled attractively for the fish to which elaborate lures to use when the worm can was empty. After we'd landed our day's catch and returned from the other side of the lake in a rowboat, he set up a cleaning station on the rocks at dockside, where he showed us how to gut and fillet fish before placing them over the fire. After a dinner of trout, catfish and potatoes baked in the glowing coals, the fisherman left us to clean his gear and pack up his station wagon. Tired and ready to fall asleep, the six of us sipped hot chocolate with our feet pressed to the firepit for added warmth. That was when the fisherman's wife stoked the fire back to life and continued to tell us the legend of Slumach's gold.

"There's an Indian curse that protects the mine from discovery." Shuddering at the thought, she pulled her shawl tighter around her shoulders. She told us about the Salish man named Slumach who was hunting deer in steep, unforgiving mountains when he stumbled upon a creek scattered with gold nuggets that had spilled from a cavern. "That was 1889," she said. "He'd bring gold nuggets the size of walnuts into New Westminster, which was two days' hard canoeing from the head of Pitt Lake. And he'd buy drinks for everyone, attracting lots of attention to himself as he bragged about his secret cache. He would boast that there were 'more nuggets where these came from.' Then he'd slip out of town with a lovely young lady as a companion."

These details tumbled around our minds as her story unfolded beside the campfire. Apparently Slumach was real, and none of what we heard seemed remotely like a myth. She continued: "Those gold seekers who tried to follow Slumach to his gold mine vanished on the dead-end trails leading into the mountains from Pitt Lake, where dense fog could appear without warning and sudden winds would churn the lake into nightmare waves."

The storyteller tossed a cedar log on the fire. Its slivers sparked, burning bright and warm right away. Still, we shivered. Fear seemed to reach out for us from the dark hillside behind her, and search for us from the star-sprinkled sky. We knew death was out there. We could feel it.

She continued: "And none of his women was ever seen alive again."

Six hearts nearly stopped beating when the old lady came to the part about the Salish man getting arrested and tried for the murder of a young woman. She had last been seen leaving town with him, and subsequently was found floating in the Fraser River with Slumach's hunting knife stuck in her back. The suspense drew us nearer the fire for safety, riveted under the spell of her story. "It was on the prison gallows that Slumach said his curse as they put a hood

On a summer evening in 1957 beside a lake much like the one shown here, the fisherman's wife spoke of the legend of Slumach, his gold and his deadly curse.

over his head and a noose around his neck. It happened just before the trapdoor sprang open and dropped Slumach to his death at the end of a five-strand rope."

We hung on her words just as surely as if the noose were strung around our own necks. Then we heard of Slumach's admonition, a phrase that would spark decades of dreams, research, adventure and writing: "Nika memloose, mine memloose." She attributed this phrase to Slumach himself, and called it "Slumach's curse." Her interpretation was rough and emphatic: "When I die, mine dies," she translated, saying he mumbled it twice to get the attention of his executioner and the witnesses. His final words were the clincher: "Anyone who finds my mine, will die because of that."

What more could young brothers want? For years, as our family left our weekend camp at the lake and drove 50 miles of narrow highway toward Vancouver and home, we'd ask Dad to slow down as the road passed through Pitt Meadows. In the distance, jagged mountains pocked with ravines and home to bears and cougars bordered Pitt Lake on the east and west. A glacier-fed river flowed into the lake's north end, and the south end fed Pitt River. Fog shrouded the cliffs and water in a mystery so deep it seemed impenetrable. Every time, we would look at one another in the back seat of the Chevrolet, point north, and then one of us would say to the other, "That's where Slumach's lost gold mine is. One day we'll go and find it. One day ..."

There was a television show in the 1950s called *Treasure*. In black and white and shadowy greys, it brought tales of adventure into our family's living room. The weekly series portrayed everything young boys found inspiring: buried pirate chests still unfound centuries later despite the existence of maps; money from a daring 19th-century bank heist in the United States that was stashed in a place so secret it has never been located, despite solid hints from dying robbers; hand-drawn sketches with directions to a missing trunk filled with valuable shares in a silver mine. The show's host would warn of the dangers that would-be explorers were sure to encounter if they ventured in search of these lost treasures.

One evening in 1958, the show featured Slumach's incredible discovery of "gold beyond your wildest dreams." The hosts said the mine still lay hidden 35 miles northeast of Vancouver—less than an hour's drive away from us. Fog foiled the film crew, descending upon them with alarming suddenness and forcing them to abandon their search. The final frames from their camera captured a narrow entrance that faded from view as the chronicler declaimed: "There ... is the entrance to the mine. We were that near ... before the curse closed in." This broadcast, of course, raised the spectre of competing gold seekers, and renewed our commitment to search every

This is Spindle Canyon, which was shown in an episode of the 1958 television show *Treasure* that featured the Slumach story. As ground fog closed in, members of the film crew had to abandon their quest to find his gold, even though they had reached what they believed was the entrance to the mine. Could the fog have been Slumach's curse at work?

nook and cranny of Pitt Lake's 40-mile shoreline—just as soon as we outgrew parental restrictions on such absurd adventures.

A more adult quest for Slumach's mine was sparked many years later when the story came up in passing conversation. From that unlikely beginning sprang a serious research project to separate fact from fiction in Pitt Lake's Lost Creek gold mine story, and to determine which parts of the Pitt Lake region Slumach might have found most promising for hunting—and thus most likely to be the site of his stumbled-upon gold mine. It would be these places where we would plan to take our canoe trips, or where we imagined ourselves hiking in Slumach's footsteps. We two veterans of the campfire story were joined by a friend, Mary Trainer, and the three of us together sought every scrap of detail available in old photographs and newspaper clippings, interviewed people who claimed to know something about the story and read turn-of-the-century documents. The motherlode

Slumach country: The glacier-fed waters of the upper Pitt River flow into Pitt Lake here. Gold seekers pass through here as they start their searches.

of information was *The Columbian*, then (in 1971) one of three daily newspapers in the Vancouver area. Reporters, foremost among them the tenacious Alan Jay, had regularly tracked and reported on the legend of Slumach's gold. While other papers, notably the *Vancouver Province*, merely suggested in one story that upward of 30 deaths were linked to Slumach's curse, *The Columbian* took their coverage much further. It even ran annual features with promotional advertising, and highlighted clues and questionable "history" that sent weekend fortune hunters perennially traipsing across open ridges and over private lands in search of Slumach's mine.

Our more serious research was welcomed in the community. British Columbia's approaching centennial year of joining Confederation, 1971, was generating media attention, and new work was being published to feed the growing appetite for stories about the lively heritage and fascinating personalities that had built the province.

Gold seekers take in the treacherously steep and dangerous country lying between them and potential gold.

Rikk Taylor, the clever and engaging publisher of *The Columbian*, supported our project. We were barely into our 20s, and penniless; he was middle-aged and successful. He fanned the embers of our interest, providing assistance wherever possible and giving us access to his paper's extensive archives, which included the original coverage of Slumach's trial. He saw in us a youthful version of his own enthusiasm, and encouraged our pursuit of Slumach's legend by covering our search in his newspaper. This in turn provided us with more leads, harder evidence and anonymous phone calls ("I have something you might be interested in ... ").

We encountered fascinating 19th-century figures in the Slumach story, people like murder victim Louis Bee, Constable Eric Grainger, and prospector R.A. "Volcanic" Brown. The result was the 1972 publication of *In Search of a Legend: Slumach's Gold*. Our slim book recounted the true story and, importantly, the embellishments and distortions to it that had been made over the years. The book contained artist Fred Bosman's rendition of a map highlighting various locations around Pitt Lake where *we* believed, based on our research, the mine might be found, *if* it existed. At one point, a Vancouver Public Library employee told us the library had to keep ordering more copies of the book because patrons would read it and, believing the map to be the real thing, abscond with it.

Within two months of our book's release, a finely researched book was published by former RCMP constable Don Waite. Its title, *Kwant'stan*, is the Salish peoples' name for the impressive Golden Ears, the snow-capped twin peaks of Mt. Blanshard, reminiscent of wolves' ears, that reflect the sun and pinpoint Pitt Lake's location. Many people have speculated that Slumach's gold is hidden within the folds of those rocky crags.

Our book and Don Waite's were amalgamated in 1981 under our original title. It was edited by Art Downs, the former publisher of *BC Outdoors* magazine and then-owner of Heritage House Publishing. Our 1972 edition, Don Waite's *Kwant'stan*, and the Heritage House edition collectively sold more than 10,000 copies and have all long been out of print. Dozens of speculative newspaper and magazine articles and at least three television documentaries have since appeared covering explorations into the region, as well as other books. Each undertaking, spurred on by "there's gold ..." ambitions, has been in the spirit of adventure; all, however, have come up empty. Yet the legend of the Lost Creek gold mine persists. We long ago determined that much of the story was a lark and that the mine probably *never* existed. Frankly, we had not given it a lot of thought over the past 35 years, except for giving media interviews now and then and answering the questions of other amateur historians. Of course, we were aware that other researchers were finding additional information and writing articles or books, or making television documentaries; we considered them fellow gold seekers.

Then one day a long-retired Rikk Taylor, whom we hadn't seen for nearly two decades, telephoned to arrange a get-together, as he had some startling news. A week later, on a fine autumn day with colours changing everywhere, two middle-aged brothers and an elderly gentleman settled into a booth at The Keg restaurant in Burnaby. Struggling with the degenerative aftermath of a stroke, Rikk spoke in a halting voice. He told us that he'd kept an eye on the Slumach story after he had left the newspaper business. Then, before our meals arrived, he made a remarkable gesture: he held up a large zip-lock bag that contained several small samples of quartz, and a rock the size of a man's fist. Pushing the parcel across the table toward us, he paused partway to open it and reach inside with a jittery hand. He retrieved two dusty sheets of paper that had been tossed around with the rocks. "It's an assay report," he said, shaking dirt off the pages.

We must have looked quite puzzled. "I want you to have all this," Rikk said, passing us the bag and the report. "The rocks contain a lot of gold." Then he began to tell his story in earnest.

"They've found Slumach's lost mine ... "

Rick Antonson, Mary Trainer
and Brian Antonson
Summer 2007

New Westminster's Columbia Street in the 1890s. The streets and saloons of this frontier town were said to be Slumach's stomping grounds.

The Legend of Slumach and His Lost Creek Gold Mine

British Columbia's rich and colourful history is alive with legends, but one of the most enduring is that of a Native man named Slumach and his Lost Creek gold mine. Of a host of variations to the legend, here is the most common:

Sometime in the late 1880s, somewhere in the mountainous country surrounding Pitt Lake and 20 miles from the bustling river port of New Westminster, a Salish Indian named Slumach stumbled on a fabulously rich outcropping of almost pure gold. His find was a glory hole. According to Slumach's stories, nuggets the size of a man's fist lay all about, and the bed of the creek abounded with gold. Slumach packed some of the metal out to civilization and began the first of many wild tours through New Westminster, spending freely in the Royal City's saloons and sporting houses. He tossed his nuggets about and gleefully watched the other patrons scramble for them, and then when his supply was gone, he disappeared from town.

Soon after, Slumach returned to New Westminster with another supply of gold, and his spending orgy resumed. Again and again he came to spend his wealth, but always disappeared without a trace as soon as his nuggets ran out. He refused to tell anyone the location of his hoard, and he successfully eluded all those who tried to follow him on his trips out of town.

Slumach often took young women with him when he went away for his gold—supposedly to assist him in recovering more nuggets. None of the women was ever seen alive again. During one of his spending sprees, Slumach met an attractive half-Irish, half-Chinese girl named Molly Tynan. She had arrived in New Westminster while Slumach was out of town and, on hearing of his wealth, announced her intentions to claim this Indian for her own when he returned. This she did, despite the warnings that eight other girls had vanished while attempting the very same thing.

Six weeks after Molly and Slumach left town for the mine, her body was found floating in the Fraser River. She had been stabbed to death, and the knife was still in her heart.

Slumach was questioned on his next trip to New Westminster, and he claimed that the girl had turned back only a day after they had left town. He said that when he had last seen her, she was heading for Vancouver. Unfortunately for Slumach, his mother had been shown the knife taken from Molly's body and had identified it as his. On this evidence, Slumach was tried and convicted of Molly's bloody murder.

Even under sentence of death, Slumach refused to reveal the location of his mine. In addition, as he stood on the gallows he whispered a curse on those who would seek it, saying that no one would ever find it and live. "Nika memloose, mine memloose" meant "When I die, mine dies." The mine's location may have died with Slumach, but his curse is very much alive.

In the spring of the following year, a San Francisco man came to New Westminster and announced he was going to find Slumach's mine. Local Natives, fearful of the curse, refused to guide him into the Pitt Lake mountains. He left alone. Five months later, he reappeared near New Westminster, a near skeleton, shivering with pain and telling of unbelievable hardships. He died a few days later as a result of his injuries—the first victim of Slumach's curse.

Since Slumach's death, his curse has claimed more than 30 lives. The country that hides his mine is rugged—in places the mountainsides are vertical, game is scarce, and landslides and avalanches are common hazards. But still, amateur and professional prospectors search for Slumach's elusive glory hole, and more than 115 years after his death, his spirit lives on to guard his secret.

So goes the legend—a story that has thrived in the hearts of hundreds, perhaps thousands, of gold seekers for over a century. Since it first captured our interest many years ago, we have spent considerable time researching this intriguing legend to find what truth, if any, lies behind its many different versions. In doing so, we have discovered more twists and turns than we thought possible—and we have found what we feel to be the truth behind it. We include here the details that were in our 1972 publication, followed by our new chapter on "gold seekers," which adds many tantalizing theories, freshly unveiled facts and plenty of reasons to keep the search for the lost mine alive.

The central figure, Slumach, certainly did live and was hanged—this much is public record. But is there evidence that points to Slumach being the owner of a secret gold mine? Or, is there so much evidence against Slumach's ownership that it would seem the legend is just that—a legend? Have those who searched for it and those who have died—as few as 11, as many as 36, depending on the report—been fools? Did they not heed the lack of evidence about Slumach's mine?

There *is* enough credible (although circumstantial) evidence to show that there may well be a treasure trove of gold in the unforgiving Pitt River country of the Coast Mountains. It might even be linked to Slumach. And some still believe it just may be protected by a curse.

The provincial jail in New Westminster was the site of Slumach's hanging.

Some Say This, Some Say That

At exactly 8 a.m. on January 16, 1891, Slumach plunged to his death on the gallows at the British Columbia provincial jail in New Westminster. One legend says that Slumach was hanged for the murder of a woman he had taken with him to help recover gold from his mine. That legend is wrong. His crime was indeed murder, but not that of a female helpmate. He was hung for the murder of Louis Bee, a half-breed whom he had shot without warning at Alouette Slough on September 8, 1890.

Many years passed before the legend of Slumach and his gold came to light. None of the newspapers of the day or the court records of his trial mention it. But by 1901, enough of a story was circulating to interest an Alaskan miner named Jackson.

Jackson arrived in New Westminster early in the spring of 1901 declaring he would find the mine, or die trying. The stories he had probably heard must have told of great wealth to be had by the person who could uncover the lost glory hole.

When the thaw came, Jackson headed into the Pitt Lake area to search for the treasure. Late in the fall, he returned to New Westminster a sick and broken man. He spoke little, and stayed only a few days before leaving for San Francisco.

Some people had noted that while he was in town, Jackson kept his packsack with him at all times, and, after his return to San Francisco, word came back that he had deposited close to $10,000 in raw gold in the Bank of British North America. Unfortunately, the great earthquake and fire of April 18, 1906, destroyed any records that could have proved this claim.

Jackson never recovered from his journey into the Pitt Lake area. After three years of sickness and declining health, he died. But he had found gold, and in a letter to a friend named Shotwell, he described his find. Shotwell, a Seattle resident, had grubstaked Jackson on some of his earlier trips, and had helped with the search for Slumach's mine. Jackson sent Shotwell a letter describing how he might find the mine.

One copy of the letter is known to have survived and was enclosed in some material belonging to Volcanic Brown dated May 28, 1924 (some 20 years after the letter was supposedly written). The following copy of Jackson's letter is reprinted courtesy of N.L. (Bill) Barlee, author/publisher of several B.C. books, including the bestselling *Gold Creeks and Ghost Towns* and *The Guide to Gold Panning*. To our knowledge, it is the only authenticated copy in existence. The letter reads:

> I had been out over two months and found myself running short of grub. I had lived mostly on fresh meat for one cant carry much of a pack in those hills. I found a few very promising ledges and colors in the little creeks but nothing I cared to stay with. I had almost made up my mind to light out the next day. I climbed up to the top of a sharp ridge and looked down into the canyon or valley about one mile and a half long, and what struck me as singular, it appeared to have no outlet for the little creek that flowed at the bottom. Afterwards I found that the creek entered a [an unintelligible word—thought by some to be subterranean tunnel] and was lost. After some difficulty I found my way down to the creek. The water was almost white, the formation for the most part had been slate and granite, but there I found a kind of schist and slate formation. Now comes the interesting part. I had only a small prospecting pan but I found colors at once right on the surface, and such colors they were. I knew then that I had struck it right at last. In going up stream I came to a place where bedrock was bare, and there, you could hardly believe me, the

bedrock was yellow with gold. Some of the nuggets was as big as walnuts and there were many chunks carrying quartz. After sizing it up, I saw there was millions stowed around in the little cracks. On account of the weight I buried part of the gold at the foot of a large tent shaped rock facing the creek. You cant miss it. There is a mark cut out in it. Taking with me what I supposed to be ten thousand dollars (in gold) but afterwards proved to be a little over eight thousand dollars.

After three days hard traveling, it would not have been over two days good going, but the way was rough and I was not feeling well, I arrived at the Lake and while resting there was taken sick and have never since been able to return, and now I fear I never shall. I am alone in the world, no relatives, no one to look after me for anything. Of course I have never spoken of this find during all this time for fear of it being discovered. It has caused me many anxious hours, but the place is so well guarded by surround ridges and mountains that it should not be found for many years, unless someone knew of it being there. O, how I wish I could go with you to show you this wonderful place, for I cannot give you any exact directions, and it may take a year or more to find. Dont give up but keep at it and you will be repaid beyond your wildest dreams. I believe any further directions would only tend to confuse it, so I will only suggest further that you go alone or at least only take one or two trusty Indians to pack food and no one need know but that you are going on a hunting trip until you find the place and get everything for yourself. When you find it and I am sure you will, should you care to see me, advertise in the "Frisco Examr.", and if I am living I will either come to see you, or let you know where to find me, but once more I say to you, dont fail to look this great property up and dont give up until you find it.

Now goodbye and may success attend you.

Yours truly,
W. Jackson

One of the reasons that this letter is thought to be authentic is its author's use of terms commonly known only to prospectors or those involved in gold prospecting. And his reference to the *"Frisco Examr."* *(San Francisco Examiner)* is worthy of note, as this was indeed one of the dailies operating in San Francisco at the time this letter was supposedly written (1904).

Though a map was later constructed from Jackson's very rudimentary directions, no map is believed to have accompanied his original correspondence, and the directions are so vague that his location could really be anywhere north of Pitt Lake.

Shotwell sold Jackson's letter to a group of Seattle businessmen, who began a search for the mine. It is possible that these men made several copies of the letter and sold it to other fortune hunters. In any case, their efforts to find the mine came to nothing.

Since those early days, many people have searched. Some used copies of Jackson's letter; others were armed with a "genuine" map bought or acquired from a secret source. One interesting aspect about such maps is that Fraser McDonald, New Westminster's gold commissioner for 22 years, reported that he had seen at least a dozen different maps, each pointing out different locations of the treasure. One enterprising American had printed thousands of maps that he sold for $12.50 each.

Various press reports have said that as few as 11 or as many as 36 people have died looking for the mine. While the figures vary, there is no question that *some* people have died during the search. If Slumach's curse is not responsible, then maybe the mine's supposed locations are. All of the suggested locales (save Sheridan Hill) are in difficult country. Many of those who have met their deaths while on the search were inexperienced people who thought they could find the mine easily by relying on their own wiles, but found the task more than they could manage. Even experienced outdoors enthusiasts find the Pitt Lake mountains difficult and dangerous.

And what of the curse itself? According to the legend, Slumach stated that what was his would die when he died, or that any who tried to find the mine would die trying, or that any who found the mine would surely die. There is no record, however, of Slumach having made this curse in any of its versions as he stood on the gallows.

Just as the curse may be a figment of someone's imagination, so could the very existence of gold in the Pitt River country. Even though estimates of the treasure have been as high as $100 million, geological surveys indicate it is an unlikely place to find gold. Tests and studies have shown that the necessary conditions for producing ore-bearing rock simply don't exist there, nor does the possibility of placer deposits. If there is a mine in the mountains, it must indeed be a glory hole, where the gold is in the form of a vein in quartz rock rather than nuggets and dust in a stream. Strong evidence of this fact is the 11 ounces of gold found in prospector Volcanic Brown's last camp.

Stories exist of a lost gold mine in this area that have nothing to do with Slumach. One article reported a Native person finding a mine in the early 1900s, and another that a miner took between $5,000 and $7,000 in gold from the Pitt Lake area every year prior to 1915.

Then there's the centuries-old Native legend, which goes like this:

> A young Indian, in search of food, paddled his canoe into Pitt Lake and beached it on an island. When the water was low, he saw the entrance to a cavern revealed at the water's edge—he was curious and so, paddled into the cavern.
>
> As his eyes grew accustomed to the darkness of the cavern, he saw a huge serpent perched on a ledge, old and feeble, and unable to move. Before the frightened Indian youth could find his way out, the serpent spoke to him, and told him to have no fear.
>
> The serpent told the youth he had been expecting him. He was the guardian of this cave, and because he was old and dying, the young brave must take his place. The young Indian asked what the cavern held that it must be guarded so. The serpent told him that deeper within the cavern there were many shiny pebbles— pebbles that must be kept from men with white skins. The serpent said that if ever such men should find the pebbles, it would bring an end to the happy life of the Indian.
>
> As the water began to rise in the cave, the old serpent placed his head on the young Indian's shoulder. Suddenly the Indian was transformed into a serpent, and before him stood an old Indian—transformed from the body of the serpent. The old man

told him that he had first entered the cave as a young man, and had guarded its secret ever since. He admonished the young serpent to ensure that no man with white skin should ever enter the cave and leave alive. And when the water reached the roof of the cave, he slipped beneath it and disappeared.

Interestingly, Pitt Lake is a tidal lake, with about a five-foot rise and fall. If Slumach knew of this legend, it may have prompted him to search for the supposed treasure, giving birth to stories of his secret gold mine. But whatever the connection is—or isn't—the legend does exist and it does concern gold at Pitt Lake.

The information about Slumach himself is as varied and contradictory as the legend that has grown around his life. Even the correct spelling of his name has been in doubt. There are several popular versions, among them Slumah, Slummack, Slumogh, and Slumock, but the most widely accepted is Slumach. Even the basic elements of the legend have been distorted over the last century.

Although he was Coast Salish, Slumach was not typical of his people. They reportedly preferred water travel, while Slumach is said to have been an avid hunter who lived mostly in the mountainous area at the south end of Pitt Lake. Some articles state that he was "a young, handsome Indian," yet one newspaper account written at the time of Louis Bee's murder suggested that since winter was coming on, Slumach would run out of food, and "being just over 80," he would be forced from his hideout in the mountains. Since there is no record of Slumach's age—or his first name, for that matter—we can only speculate. Between 60 and 80 seems about the best guess.

One aspect of Slumach's life, however, is not speculation: before he murdered Louis Bee, he must have done little worthy of note, because prior to that event his life was unchronicled. We can assume that the press of the day would have noted any spending sprees involving raw gold and young women disappearing. They didn't.

The Murder of Louis Bee

The most reliable information on Slumach is found in the press records of 1890–91. The following material is from the *Daily Columbian*, New Westminster, B.C. It was compiled for the periodical, *The Native Voice*, in July 1959, by William W. Burton:

The Daily Columbian
September 9, 1890

SHOT DEAD

Louis Bee, a half-breed, is deliberately shot and killed by an insane Indian named Slumach, at Lillooet Slough.

A terrible unpremeditated murder was committed yesterday afternoon at a point on Lillooet Slough, not far from the Pitt River, and some two and a half miles above the Pitt River Bridge. An Indian named Slumach, aged about sixty years, was hunting in this neighborhood, and coming out of the bush with his double-barreled shotgun in his hand, found several other Indians trout-fishing on the banks of the Slough.

A half-breed named Louis Bee, sauntered up to Slumach and asked him in a casual way what he was shooting around there.

Without a moment's warning, or any preliminary sign of anger, Slumach instantly leveled his gun at Bee and fired.

Just before the discharge of the piece, Bee held up his hands and begged Slumach not to shoot. The distance between the two men was so short that the whole charge entered the victim's body, just under the right armpit, behind the shoulder-blade. Death was instantaneous, and Bee fell without a groan and lay weltering in his blood, while his murderer coolly proceeded to reload his piece.

One of the Indians who witnessed the awful deed immediately fled, not only to give the alarm, but from motives of personal safety. He describes the countenance of the murderer after the act was committed as resembling that of an incarnate demon. Slumach is insane, and what he had done seemed to have kindled all the wild disorderly fancies of madness in the maniac's brain, and lit up his eyes with a ferocious gleam that boded no good to anyone whom he should encounter when his gun was reloaded. Slumach slowly retreated to the impenetrable and pathless jungle surrounding that part of the Lillooet Slough and plunging into its gloomy recesses was lost to sight and is still at large.

September 10, 1890

THE MURDER OF LOUIS BEE

Through the courtesy of Mr. L.F. Bonson, who placed his fine steam launch at the coroner's disposal, Capt. Pittendrigh and his attendants were enabled to perform the journey yesterday from the city to the scene of the Indian murder at Pitt River, in an expeditious and comfortable manner. Long before the fatal spot was reached, the Indians could be heard chanting a loud strange death song, or coronach, for the untimely demise of their comrade Louis Bee. The party from the city, on arriving at the place where the murder occurred, found a number of Indians congregated together, and apparently suffering from fear to a considerable extent.

Enquiry developed the fact that none of them dared to pursue the murderer through the bush, and their terror increased by the appearance of Slumach the day following the murder and his appropriation of the murdered man's remains. He placed the body in a canoe and set out in the direction of the lake with it. It was suspected that Slumach's intention was to drop the body overboard in the deep water, and Capt. Pittendrigh, acting on the supposition, set the Indians to work dragging the river for the corpse. The latest news received states that the body was recovered, and was in the custody of friends in the neighborhood of the spot where the tragic occurrence happened.

The Indian eyewitness who came to the city with the first information of the crime, was taken to the city lock-up this morning for safekeeping by order of Mr. W. Moresby.

Capt. Pittendrigh and jury returned from the Pitt River last night. This morning a new jury was summoned to proceed to view the remains of Bee.

September 11, 1890

CORONER'S INQUEST

A coroner's inquest was held yesterday in the committee rooms at the City Hall upon the body of Louis Bee, the half-breed who was murdered last Monday afternoon at Pitt River by an Indian named Slumach, and whose remains were brought to the city yesterday. Dr. Walker performed the post-mortem examination, and found the bone of the upper left arm to have been shattered by the passage of a ball, which had entered the side of the deceased, fracturing the fifth rib, penetrated the right side of the heart, and torn the lungs. The bullet was found embedded in the right lung. Death, in the doctor's opinion, must have been instantaneous. Charlie Seymour, an Indian, was the principal witness examined by the jury.

The jury returned the verdict of willful murder against the Indian Slumach.

The body of the murdered man was coffined, and taken home by the Indians for interment at their own cemetery near the entrance to Pitt Lake. Mr. Moresby and two special officers left this morning by steamer for the scene of the murder.

They were to be met by the Chief of the Indians with a selected posse of men, and the search for Slumach will be prosecuted unceasingly until he is captured.

September 12, 1890

STILL AT LARGE

Slumach, the murderer of Louis Bee is still at large, and there is no immediate prospect of his capture, unless he is driven by starvation into the haunts of men. Mr. Moresby went up to Pitt Lake yesterday and continued the search for him, but with no success. Just before Mr. Moresby arrived, the Indians saw Slumach at his cabin, but he quickly plunged into the bush again and was not visible during the remainder of the day. On examining the cabin, Mr. Moresby found a can of powder and a large quantity of provisions, which he destroyed, and then to prevent Slumach returning there for shelter, the shack was burned to the ground. His canoe was also destroyed.

Slumach will now have to keep to the woods until cold weather and starvation drives him in. Mr. Moresby left for Pitt Lake again this morning and may not return to the city for several days. He is determined to bring him to justice, and will, if he can, obtain the assistance required.

The Indians are all afraid of the murderer, and decline to assist in beating the bush for him, as he is well armed and has lots of ammunition. Slumach is a desperate character and is credited by the Indians with another murder, committed years ago and under similar circumstances. Although a few of the murderer's friends say he is insane, dozens of the Indians who know him, say otherwise, and declared he is only a bloodthirsty old villain.

September 16, 1890

SLUMACH THE MURDERER STILL AT LARGE

Indians who know him well, say he has committed four or five murders during the last 25 years.

His last murder, previous to the killing of Louis Bee, was committed about six years ago when he is said to have killed an Indian without any apparent cause. He fled to the mountains and remained in seclusion for a whole year, and then suddenly returned one day and took possession of his cabin and lived quietly until the perpetration of his last crime.

Slumach is looked upon by the Indians as a very wonderful person, being able to endure the greatest hardships without apparent inconvenience. As a hunter he is without an equal, and he is adept at making fires in the primitive manner, using two sticks and rubbing the same together until the friction ignites the wood. He is said to be without fear of man or beast and to be possessed of a nature vicious in the extreme.

September 19, 1890—(No Heading)

Mr. W. Moresby went up to Pitt Lake on the steamer Constance on Wednesday, returning to the city last night. Constable

Anderson reported having seen Slumach the preceding day, standing on a rocky bluff afar off with nothing on but a red shirt and a handkerchief tied around his head.

He was armed with his deadly rifle, and was too far away to permit of an exchange of bullets. On the nearer approach of his pursuers he quietly retreated into the impregnable fastnesses among the stupendous precipices that frown over the lake at that neighbourhood. He has not since been seen.

September 19, 1890

SLUMACH'S ACTION

The Indians say that Slumach has always acted strangely, and at irregular intervals would withdraw himself alone into the forests that border for weeks, reappearing at the end of those periods of abberration looking haggard, and more like a savage beast than a human being. In spite of his lunacy however, the maniac never displayed any signs of hostility, nor gave indications that his freedom was dangerous to human life.

He is described as a very powerful man and is rather dreaded by his own Indian friends.

It is of the utmost importance that fishing and hunting parties going into this region, should keep a most vigilant lookout, as the murderer is still roaming the woods armed with a shotgun, and as far as can be learned, with plenty of ammunition.

The Indian who informed Mr. McTiernan, Indian Agent, of the occurrence, says that from Slumach's looks, he had not the slightest doubt that he would murder the first man he met.

Parties contemplating a visit to the spot indicated above should therefore be on their guard, as carelessness in this matter may result in a still more lamentable tragedy than that just described.

Louis Bee was a splendid specimen of the half-breed, he was tall, well-informed, and very muscular, besides having a rather handsome face. It is related of him that once, when in the city, and under the influence of liquor, six stalwarts could not hold him down, and it was only by their dogged perseverance that they at length got him to the police office. ·

Bee figured several times in police court, owing to his fondness for alcoholic stimulants, but otherwise he was a quiet respectable man.

Several parties of men are now scouring the woods in the neighbourhood of the scene of the murder, in the endeavor to run the desperate perpetrator of the crime to earth.

The Indians in that part of the district are intensely excited over the horrible affair, and are doing everything in their power to capture Slumach.

October 25, 1890

STARVED OUT

The Indian Slumach, who attained to ghastly celebrity some weeks ago by wantonly murdering a young half-breed named Louis Bee, has been suffering terrible privations in the mountain fastnesses around the shores of Pitt Lake, whither he retired after the murder and set the power of the law at defiance. A month ago, Mr. P. McTiernan, Indian Agent here, had a conference with the members of the tribe at Pitt Lake, and succeeded in convincing them of their duty to deliver Slumach over to the law. From that day no assistance was given to the outlaw, and probably on that account was he forced to give himself up yesterday to the police. Yesterday he sent his nephew for the Indian Agent, who went up to Pitt Lake accompanied by two Indian policemen, and to them the desperate fugitive quietly surrendered. He had eaten nothing for several days, and was in a terrible state of emaciation and thoroughly exhausted.

His ammunition was all gone and his clothing in rags, and he presented a very wild and weatherworn aspect.

Slumach was at once brought to the city and placed under the care of the physicians of the Provincial jail.

At latest account today, Slumach was in a very precarious condition, his vitality being spent. The doctors do not care to express an opinion as to his chances of recovery, but it is understood that they are very small. Should he recover he will be given a preliminary trial, and then remanded for trial at the assizes in November.

November 3, 1890

DISTRICT COURT

(Before Capt. Pittendrigh, JP)

The murderer, Slumach, was up in the district court before Capt. Pittendrigh, JP, for a preliminary hearing. Several witnesses were examined, and a mass of evidence taken down, and the magistrate sent Slumach up for trial at the approaching assizes.

The prisoner has greatly improved in health since his surrender and will be strong enough to undergo the tedium of the assize trial this month. Slumach is rather an intelligent looking man of about sixty years of age. His face expressed a great deal of determination, even ferocity. He sat in court listening to the evidence this morning with the utmost apathy.

A number of Indians occupied seats and took a great deal of interest in the proceedings.

Above: Captain George Pittendrigh, JP, led the team that recovered Louis Bee's body and brought it back to New Westminster.

November 11, 1890

THE CASE OF SLUMACH

Slumach, the murderer of Louis Bee, now confined in the Provincial goal [*sic*] awaiting trial at the Assizes which opens to-morrow, is in a very bad state of health, and may not be in a fit condition to appear for trial at this term. He is very weak and does not seem to gather strength so rapidly as might be expected, considering the attention and comforts he receives from the medical superintendent and gaol officials.

Mr. McTiernan, Indian Agent, is of the opinion that Slumach will not live long in confinement, and it is a well known fact that an Indian sentenced to a long term of imprisonment soon pines away and dies. It now looks as if Slumach will not be able to stand trial at the coming assizes, and should this turn out to be the case it is pretty certain that he will escape the gallows by death from natural causes before the spring term.

November 14, 1890

FALL ASSIZES

Court resumed sittings at 10:30 o'clock.

The crown prosecutor asked the arraignment of Slumach for murder. Mr. T.C. Anderson, defending counsel asked that this case be adjourned until next assizes, on the ground that there were two important witnesses for the defence, Moody, an Indian and Florence Reed, who could not possibly be obtained in time for this assize, but could be produced at the next sitting of the court. The affidavits of Slumach and his daughter Mary, were produced and read ...

Mr. Moresby said he could produce the witnesses required by the defence by 11 o'clock tomorrow, and his Lordship therefore adjourned the court until that time.

November 15, 1890

FALL ASSIZES

(Mr. Justice Drake presiding)

The Slumach murder case occupied the attention of the court today. The evidence had to be nearly all interpreted.

There were several Indian witnesses examined at length, and they gave minute particulars of the tragedy.

It came out in the evidence that Bee, the victim of the murder, was in the habit of blustering at, and threatening almost everyone with whom he came in contact. Against Slumach he indulged something like a grudge, and for a long time there was bad blood between them. The Indians who were with Bee at the time of the murder were fishing, and on Slumach emerging from the adjacent woods, a slight altercation ensued between him and Bee, with the result that Slumach shot him dead.

The jury retired at 3:45, and after being out 15 minutes, returned with a verdict of guilty.

His Lordship sentenced Slumach to be hanged on Jan. 16 next.

Above: Justice Montague William Tyrwhitt Drake presided at Slumach's trial in 1890, sentencing him to death on November 15.

January 16, 1891

PAID THE PENALTY

Slumach, the murderer of Louis Bee, pays the penalty of his crime. Old Slumach was hanged in the yard of the provincial gaol this morning at 8 o'clock, for the murder on Sept. 8th last, of Louis Bee, a half-breed.

The particulars of the hanging are briefly as follows ... Pierre, (the Indian catechist-medicine man) slept in the same cell with Slumach, and prayed with him day and night and it is satisfactory to know that the labor of the good priest and his assistant was not in vain ...

The condemned man retired to rest at an early hour last night and slept well...

Slumach awakened early and immediately went into devotional exercises with his spiritual attendants, after which breakfast was brought in and he ate a good meal with apparent relish.

A few minutes before 7 o'clock, Father Morgan baptized Slumach, who professed his belief in Christianity and the hope of salvation. Prayers were continued until the arrival of the hangman to pinion him, and to this operation he submitted without a murmur. All being in readiness a few minutes before 8 o'clock, the procession was formed and proceeded to the scaffold. Mr. Sheriff Armstrong led the way followed by Mr. Wm. Moresby, governor of the jail and the deputy sheriff, next came Slumach, supported by gaolers Burr and Connor, and followed by the hangman, masked and hooded.

Father Morgan, Pierre, Dr. J.M. McLean, Dr. Walker and a number of constables brought up the rear of the procession.

Slumach walked firmly up the steps leading to the platform, and faced the crowd below. The hangman quickly adjusted the noose, and Father Morgan commenced a prayer. Then the black cap put on, and at 8 o'clock exactly, the bolt was drawn, the trap fell, and Slumach had paid the penalty of his crime.

The hanging was very ably managed and beyond a few little twitchings of the hands and feet, the body remained perfectly still after the drop. In three minutes and fifty-eight seconds life was pronounced extinct, but it was more than twenty minutes before the body was cut down and placed in the coffin.

Coroner Pittendrigh and a jury viewed the body and brought in the usual verdict. Slumach's neck was broken in the fall, and death must have been painless. The drop was eight feet, five inches. Over fifty persons witnessed the hanging, and a large crowd gathered outside the jail, and remained there until the black flag was hoisted. Among the crowd on the street were several Indian women, relatives of Slumach, who waited around the jail more than an hour after the execution

New Westminster just after the Great Fire of September 10, 1898. Many records were destroyed in this fire, including Captain Pittendrigh's, some of which were probably related to Slumach's case.

The Legend Is Born

Nowhere in these newspaper reports is there any mention of gold, nor is there any conclusive evidence that Slumach had murdered anyone other than Louis Bee. And with the hanging, the press's interest in the life of Slumach ended.

Why did he murder Louis Bee? Where did the original legends about his gold originate if he really had none? These questions and others open up a new angle on Slumach's life—one that is not documented by public records, but which has been widely recounted.

There is information that Louis Bee had been taunting Slumach before his murder by calling him a witch. This apparently was one of the worst slurs anyone could make to an Aboriginal person, and this may have been what enraged Slumach to the point of murder.

Various articles have claimed they profile Slumach's real life just prior to Louis Bee's murder, and some even have included pictures of Slumach and his supposed female victims. Of course, there is no authoritative documentation to back up these stories, and there is no mention in the contemporary press or in the record of his trial that speaks to any of these supposed activities. We must therefore presume that these records have been compiled without the benefit of authentication. Because Slumach did not come into the public light until Bee's murder, and because the legend of his gold did not appear until many years after his death, much of the material about him is likely fabrication. There are, however, some interesting points about these fabrications—and the consequences.

The names Susan Jesner, Molly Tynan, Tillie Malcom and Mary Warne have come up frequently in the stories of Slumach's mine. They were identified as four of those who died at Slumach's hand after they had accompanied him into the Pitt Lake country to search for his gold. Unfortunately, there is no police record of these names, so it is virtually impossible to document their existence after more than a century has gone by. And it would be just as difficult to establish a connection between them and Slumach.

Nor is there anything in the Slumach trial records about the supposed murders of the women he had taken with him on his trips for gold. One entry in the trial judge's bench book states that other Native people feared him, while a report in the press said they knew he had killed others before Bee, but there is no evidence to associate him with other murders.

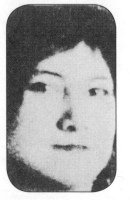

These photos of Slumach's supposed victims were widely published and identified as (top, left to right) Mary Warne, Tillie Malcom and (bottom) Susan Jesner. Where these pictures originated and whether the names attached to them are correct is unknown, but modern research casts much doubt on their authenticity.

There are many *undocumented* accounts of Slumach's actions before he murdered Louis Bee, and each one tells basically the same tale: Slumach made repeated trips into the Pitt Lake country, each time returning with a quantity of gold nuggets, which he used to pay for wild orgies in the saloons and entertainment centres of early New Westminster. His repulsive countenance proved to be no deterrent to young women, for they flocked to his side as he spent his gold, and each time he left New Westminster, one young woman left with him, and was never seen alive again.

Most of these stories end with Slumach being hanged for the murder of Molly Tynan or Susan Jesner, his most frequently named victims. Some say that the murders stopped when he was captured after Louis Bee's murder. Still, none can explain the complete lack of public press coverage of Slumach's storied orgies paid for by pure gold nuggets, and it is a dead certainty that any such expenditure would rate front-page coverage in the gold-fevered spirit of those times.

New stories or old, all paint the same basic picture of Slumach as a "bloodthirsty old villain" who somehow ended up in the middle of a thrilling legend about cursed gold, and found a place in history.

This rustic cabin is typical of those built by prospectors throughout B.C.

Theories, Theories, Theories

If the unwitting main character in the lost mine legend really had no gold, then no further discussion is required. If he *did* have gold, then a great deal more is necessary—particularly on the question of where he got it. If he did have gold, he must have obtained it in one of two ways: either from a mine, or by other, probably illegal, means. Let us assume that Slumach had no mine. Where else could he have acquired his gold? Several suggestions have been made.

Suppose it was true that Slumach took women into the bush with him to help recover his fortune. It has been suggested that Slumach and his women headed straight north, then east, winding up on the route that many Cariboo gold-rush miners had followed to New Westminster in the 1860s—down Harrison Lake. Nuggets such as those mentioned in the legend were often taken from Cariboo deposits.

According to one theory, Slumach's women would waylay miners travelling along this route, enticing them with offers of physical pleasure. When their attentions were diverted from their gold, Slumach would murder them, and, together with his female partner, make off with it.

Miners did disappear during the Cariboo gold rush—some simply vanished and others were murdered, although there was remarkably little violent crime. The main problem with the murder theory, however, is that the Harrison route to the Cariboo was short-lived.

In 1863 the Cariboo Wagon Road through the Fraser Canyon was completed, and, because the Wagon Road was far more convenient, the Harrison route was abandoned.

Another theory involves the robbery in the late 1880s of a gold-laden wagon train just north of Hope. Five men staged the holdup; one was an Aboriginal man. This would not be significant were it not that three of the White robbers were subsequently murdered, while the fourth White man and the Aboriginal man disappeared. It was reported that the latter escaped with a sizable portion of the loot, which he buried in a secret location near New Westminster. Apparently, this man was named Slumach, and he made repeated trips to this cache for more gold.

Yet another theory involves another Native man, "Hunter Jack," a chief of the Lakes Lillooet Band. On early maps of the Bridge River mining camp, there is a spot marked "Hunter Jack's Landing," close to the old Lorne Mine, which later became the Bralorne Mine. Hunter Jack lived near Shalalth and frequently made trips to New Westminster laden with gold from his diggings. Old-timers in Lillooet claim that Hunter Jack got his gold from Tyaughton Creek in the Bridge River country, an area first explored in 1858 during the stampede to the Fraser River. Hardrock claims were staked in the 1890s and eventually two mines were started, Pioneer Gold and Bralorne. Pioneer closed in the late 1950s after yielding more than 1.3 million ounces of gold, and Bralorne closed in 1971 after yielding nearly 3 million ounces. At the then-rate of $32 an ounce, this gold was worth over $120 million; today's price equivalent would be billions of dollars.

Hunter Jack was somewhat possessive about his area, and anyone who intruded could expect a confrontation. Once, a group of Chinese miners who invaded his preserve was chased out at gunpoint. To demonstrate his authority, Hunter Jack followed the miners to a river. There he charged a fee to transport them across in his boat.

Hunter Jack occasionally held potlatches at which he gave handfuls of nuggets to his guests. Slumach was a friend of Hunter Jack's

Seen here are early gold seekers working a claim in the Cariboo goldfields in 1868. Even though Cariboo creeks yielded tens of millions of dollars in gold, there was little major crime, and the few robberies that did occur were well documented. Because of this, the theory that Slumach used young women to waylay Cariboo miners seems unlikely. And since the main method of shipping gold was by stagecoach, not freight wagon, another theory that has Slumach robbing his gold from a wagon train above Hope also appears doubtful.

and probably a guest at his potlatches, so he would have regularly received quantities of nuggets. It has been rumoured that Slumach cached the gold he received from Hunter Jack in a secret location near Pitt Lake from which he drew his supply, claiming it was a secret "mine."

These theories show other possible sources for Slumach's gold than a mine, but the existence of a mine stands foremost in the common versions of the legend.

Is There a Motherlode?

Perhaps the most commonly accepted theoretical location for the mine is Sheridan Hill, a rocky outcropping north of Pitt Meadows. Before Dutch settlers moved into the Pitt Meadows and Pitt Polder areas and diked the marsh for land reclamation, Sheridan Hill stood in the middle of a slough variously known as Alouette or Lillooet Slough. Sheridan Hill was then called Menzies Isle. It had long been a sacred place in Native legends, and had figured in old stories about deposits of gold. There is an old shaft on the hill, which led many to believe that this was indeed the location. Slumach could have stored gold there and gone back for more when he needed it. Moreover, the scene of Louis Bee's murder is less than two miles from the hill.

In 1961, Sheridan Hill figured prominently in a small-scale gold rush after Wally Lund of Haney "saw" the location of Slumach's mine in a dream and contacted Elmer McLellan, editor of New Westminster's *British Columbian*. Lund pinpointed the location as being on Sheridan Hill, just a few miles north of the Lougheed Highway in Pitt Meadows. For a few weeks *The Columbian* ran stories about this latest search for the mine. Editor McLellan staked a claim at the site, and several hundred people journeyed to the scene one weekend to watch the goings-on. But "the stuff that dreams are made of" proved to be something other than gold. The would-be prospectors found that the hill had been worked several years earlier, presumably in the hope that it was the mine's secret location, but searches failed to reveal any yellow metal. Since 1961, Sheridan Hill has been an occasional stop for sightseers who still believe that somewhere in the depths of the rock, Slumach's mine lies waiting to be uncovered.

North of Sheridan Hill and across Pitt Lake on the west shore lie Widgeon Creek and Widgeon Lake, two other possible sites of the treasure. And the notation "Location of Slumach's lost mine," pointing to Widgeon Lake, was at one time on a wall map displayed in the beverage room of the Wild Duck Inn, on the Pitt River in Port Coquitlam, but very little hard information is available to support that statement.

Up Pitt Lake, other possible mine locations come into view. None has really attracted much attention. In fact, the most likely location of the mine is on Corbold Creek, more than 20 miles north of Pitt Lake.

Corbold Creek (once known as Canyon Creek) figures prominently in two searches for Slumach's mine—the 1901 search made by Jackson, and the searches made in the 1920s by Volcanic Brown.

Jackson described his find as being about 20 miles north of the lake. The parties using maps based on his letter found themselves at Corbold Creek when they began their trips. One of these parties included Captain Moore, a Victoria barrister, who gave an account published in the *Vancouver Province* in 1952. Moore said he accompanied a party to Canyon Creek in the fall of 1904. His employer, W. MacDonald, had obtained a map from a nurse, who in turn had received it from a dying prospector whom she had attended in California. Some have speculated that this prospector was Jackson.

The map used by the Moore party must have been fairly accurate from a geographical standpoint. "Following the course laid down on the map," noted Moore, "the party turned off to follow a creek that came into the Pitt from the left. We named it Canyon Creek, as the greater length of it appeared to be between precipitous hills. But as this was shown on the map, we knew we were to follow this stream to a point where we could take our bearings from three mountain peaks.

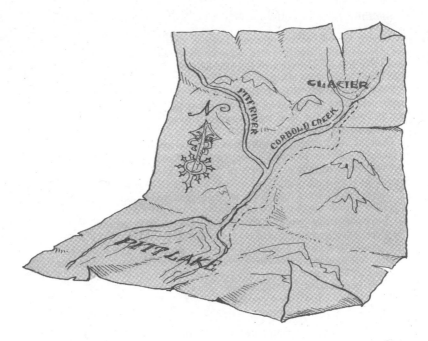

This sketch is of a map supposedly drawn by Jackson for Shotwell, the Seattle man who grubstaked him. Various versions of such a map have circulated for years.

"We did so. We found the place. There correctly drawn. But, evidently the story of the gold was a figment of his imagination—probably induced by the find that carried him off. In his delirium I fancy, he pictured the spot as being rich."

This account does not quite match the directions given in the copy of Jackson's letter, but it does lend credence to the existence of Jackson and to his discovery of gold in this area.

A great deal of research and writing on the Slumach lost gold mine story was done by Alan Jay when he was a reporter-columnist for *The Columbian*. Jay's research provided an interesting item concerning two unpublicized victims of Slumach's supposed curse.

The first was an experienced prospector in the 1950s named Alfred Gaspard. Gaspard reasoned that one of the main obstacles to finding the mine was the rough terrain in which it was located. He felt that Slumach's legendary curse worked so well because the terrain presented very difficult and dangerous situations that could easily lead to a lonely death, even without help from a curse. So to avoid having to move through too much dangerous country, Gaspard flew into a small lake in his search area and established a base camp equipped with a radio link to the outside world. He began systematic exploration of the valleys and mountains in the area. At one time he reported that he felt he was nearing the actual location of the mine, and should find it for certain within a few days. Shortly after this, he failed to report as scheduled. A search was organized, partially paid for by an emergency search fund Gaspard had provided to pay for helicopters in case he failed to rendezvous. The search continued for several weeks, but no trace was ever found of him.

The other victim was named "Tiny" Allen, who stood more than six feet high and packed more pounds than he should have on his frame. During the 1960s, Allen worked year-round as an odd-job man at the Port Arms Hotel in Port Moody. Each summer, he set out on trips into the Pitt Lake area to search for Slumach's mine. With information garnered from *The Columbian*'s file, he narrowed his search. One day he contacted Alan Jay to report that he had found the long-lost mine's location. He described the valley he had seen, saying that much of the gold was in cracks in the wall of the valley, but that most of it appeared to be down in the creek bed at the bottom. Snow and ice had prevented him from reaching the valley floor, but he was elated at actually having seen into the glory hole. Jay noted a similarity between Allen's description of the mine and the description contained in the letter sent by Jackson to his benefactor describing his find. He mentioned it to Allen, but Allen had never seen a copy of the letter. Jay showed him one, and Allen's reaction was jubilant—the two descriptions were almost identical.

The clincher was Allen's description of a huge rock that can be seen inside the mine. He said it was shaped like an Egyptian pyramid—with its top cut off. Jackson's letter refers to a large tent-shaped rock under which he buried some of the gold he had found. Allen

This sketch is of the tent-shaped rock described by Tiny Allen. (Interestingly, this image closely matches the photos taken by Norm, one of the gold seekers described further on.)

claimed he had seen this exact site and had rediscovered the mine that so many had searched for, for so long.

Allen intended to return as soon as the snow in the area had melted to allow safe access to the gold. For one reason or another, his journey was delayed for a year. The next spring, Jay attempted to contact him, only to discover he had died during the winter—the victim of a heart attack. A sister in Vancouver had handled Allen's funeral and had taken all of his possessions.

Jay contacted Allen's sister, but she refused to discuss the matter of the mine. Allen had told Jay that he had drawn a map showing the route to it; his sister denied any knowledge of the map. Jay notes that some months later he heard of a new expedition being launched to search for the mine—a search financed by three Vancouver women, using a recent map of the mine's location. No results of that search have ever come to light.

In the 1950s, an unnamed millionaire from eastern Canada hired a private investigator named Roger Gallant to research the Slumach lost mine story and report to him on the feasibility of launching a search for the mine. After inspecting all available sources, Gallant returned with the verdict that the mine did not exist, and the venture would not be worth the investment.

Another search involves a group of businessmen believed to be operating from a copy of Jackson's letter. They employed the services of Hugh Murray, a scout, stagecoach driver and prospector, to locate the mine. Murray led several expeditions into the Pitt Lake mountains, starting in 1912, but found nothing. He reported meeting an old Native woman on one of his trips. The woman told about once meeting a man in the same region who carried a pack full of gold. She said his name was Jackson, and her timing of the incident put the date back in the days when Jackson would have been fighting his way back to civilization after striking it rich.

Chief Kwikwetlem William claimed to have known Slumach, and he showed various gold seekers where to search for Slumach's "glory hole" in the dangerous country surrounding Pitt Lake.

There have been several such cases where local Native people have given information concerning the mine's location; but it has been suggested that the Native person loves to "put on" the White person—and for good reason. The White person is usually gullible and easy to fool. Perhaps these Native people have enjoyed a hearty laugh at the wild forages undertaken by White people to find a gold mine that exists only in the Native people's disingenuous tales.

Yet another attempt to find the mine was made in 1952, this time by some reporters from the *Vancouver Province*. They were led to the supposed site of the mine by Tommy William, grandson of Chief Kwikwetlem William, a Coast man who claimed he knew Slumach. Tommy said that his grandfather had led him to the site years before, and that he in turn would lead a team of reporters there. The area was covered with several feet of snow at the time, and its exploration

Seen here is one of many tent-shaped rocks investigated by gold seekers searching for Jackson's "find." Many similar rocks, of varying sizes, have been reported in a number of search areas.

proved very difficult. The following year a company named Slumach Lost Creek Mine Limited was formed that carried out an extensive and thorough search. The company published a prospectus in the *Vancouver Province* and offered 400,000 shares at a price of 12½ cents per share. This worked out to $50,000 capital on the first offering, with an authorized issue of 3,000,000 shares.

The following advice was included in their advertisement: "This is purely a speculative issue. The risk is great but it could be that the reward may be greater."

The group used helicopters and staked claims throughout the area shown them by the chief's grandson. Then, after a summer of intensive but fruitless searching, they acknowledged their defeat in the back pages of *The Province*. Nothing further was ever heard of their venture.

On July 23, 1960, the *Vancouver Sun* carried this story:

U.S. MAN DIES HUNTING GOLD—LOST MINE'S 23RD VICTIM

A vacation spent in the Pitt River badlands, hunting a legendary gold mine, ended in death for an American naval draughtsman Wednesday.

[The] body of Lewis E. Hagbo, 49, of Bremerton, Wash., was brought out to civilization Friday afternoon by a rescue party led by Sgt. Jackson Payne of the Port Coquitlam RCMP detachment.

Hagbo is the twenty-third man to die seeking the Lost Creek mine. Some died by accident, by misadventure, by exposure and by murder.

The rugged jungle of rockfall and mountain north of Pitt River is supposed to hide the Lost Creek Gold Mine. It is said that the mine, in a hidden valley, was found by the Indian Slumach, who was hanged at New Westminster in 1891.

In the past 70 years, hundreds of prospectors and hopeful adventurers have hunted the gold but none have found it.

Although Hagbo's body was found at the bottom of a cliff, he was the victim of a heart attack rather than a fall. Nevertheless, the fact that his misfortune came while he was looking for the supposed mine earned him a headline. Over the years, similar headlines in other papers such as "Fortune still elusive" (*Victoria Colonist*), "The incurable Slumach gold mine disease" (*Vancouver Province*) and "Curse Guards This Lost Gold Mine" (*Winnipeg Free Press*) have ensured that the Slumach legend remains fresh.

There is evidence that one person at least *did* find the lost gold mine. His name was Volcanic Brown, and of all those who have searched for Slumach's gold, he is the best known.

Brown's story came to light in the 1920s. Seeking refuge from a storm one night, Brown spent time with four businessmen from the town of Nelson who were on a hunting expedition. He told them that he had stumbled upon Slumach's granddaughter some years before as she lay near death on a trail. Known for his prowess as a herbalist, he succeeded in saving the woman's life. As a reward, she told him the mine's secret location.

Brown had discovered several famous mines in the Kootenays in eastern British Columbia, but the challenge of Slumach's mine led him to the coast. For several years he combed the mountains surrounding Pitt Lake searching for the mine. There is a rumour that he deposited several thousand dollars in gold nuggets in a Seattle bank, in an account held in his sister's name.

Late in the 1920s Brown went in for his annual search, and was followed by two other men. He had watched their campfire smoke some distance behind him for several days, and when he didn't see it for two days in a row, he assumed that some mishap must have overcome his followers. He decided to turn back and, after a few days, found one of the men injured on the trail. His partner had left him to go back for help, but Brown decided to help the injured man back out to civilization rather than leave him there to wait for help. Doing so put his search behind schedule, and he was late coming out of the mountains that year. The first snows caught him, and when his feet froze, he was forced to cut off most of his toes with his hunting

Volcanic Brown is seen here recuperating at the Alvin Fish Hatchery after he was carried out from Seven Mile Creek Glacier in November 1928. Then over 80 years old, he had amputated one of his toes and trimmed others because they had frozen while he was on the glacier.

The Volcanic Brown rescue party, 1928. Left to right: Herman Gardner, B.C. Provincial Policeman; Spud Murphy; Alvin Patterson, after whom Alvin was named; Caleb Gardner; Harry Corder.

knife. A search party found him and carried him to safety, but the dauntless Brown returned in 1931.

Having lost most of his toes, his movement was seriously hampered. That year, when he again failed to return, another rescue team was organized and, after 27 days of searching, two members of the party found Brown's last camp high on an icefield near the headwaters of the Stave River. His tent, cooking gear, books and prospecting materials were all in place, as if he had just left camp for a moment. But Brown himself was never found. Officials assumed he had gotten lost in a snowstorm or possibly fallen down one of the hundreds of crevasses on the Stave Glacier.

The March 20, 1932, edition of the *Province* reported on this unsuccessful search for Brown. Among those who searched was game warden George Stevenson, who said, "It was slow going—three or four miles a day. Our 12 by 48 [inch] snowshoes would sink to our knees, even without our packs. I've never seen it snow so thick and fast anywhere; we couldn't see a yard sometimes. Cold? Well, at night in the open we couldn't sleep much—had to keep up a fire. LeRoy [one of the searchers] was great, ready for anything and wouldn't say quit. We hoped Brown was snowed up somewhere, and so we fired single shots regularly, but everything was as still as the dead."

The most interesting thing found in Brown's last camp was a glass jar containing 11 ounces of raw gold, proof that somewhere on his last trip, Volcanic Brown had found gold. The metal had been hammered out of a solid vein, an indication that there must have been much more where it came from. (There are stories that Brown was seen years after his disappearance leading a very comfortable life in California, creating speculation that he had found the lost mine and had left his last camp as a decoy.)

Was Volcanic Brown another of the dozens who have died as a result of Slumach's curse? Is Jackson one of them? How many have really died while searching for the hidden fortune? And if there is gold, where will it be found? Though much evidence suggests there is no mine, just as much evidence cries out that gold has been found by more than one person in the Pitt Lake area.

The gold fever that keeps people interested was aptly summed up in an article by *The Columbian* historian John Pearson: "The only thing that could kill the legend of Slumach's lost gold mine is the discovery of the elusive cache ... "

For their own sake, however, people enticed into the Pitt River region by visions of a $100-million motherlode should proceed cautiously and heed the words of one veteran prospector: "That has to be the worst topographical area in the province."

Still, in spite of the dangers, fortune hunters go looking for Slumach's lost mine year after year.

This sketch is of Volcanic Brown's last camp, high on the Stave Glacier. Exactly where Brown's last camp was remains unknown.

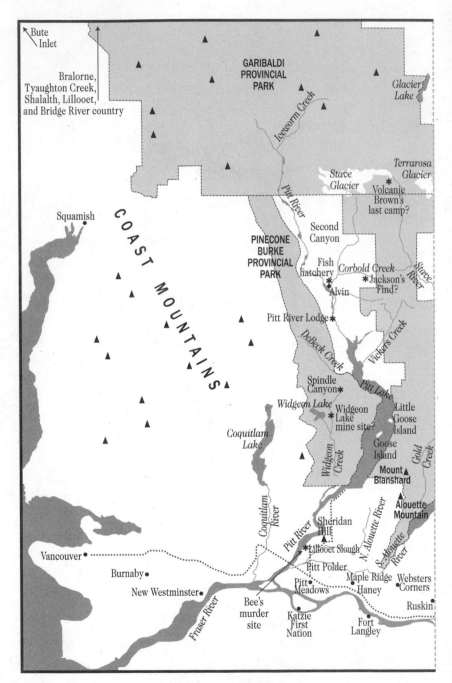

SLUMACH COUNTRY

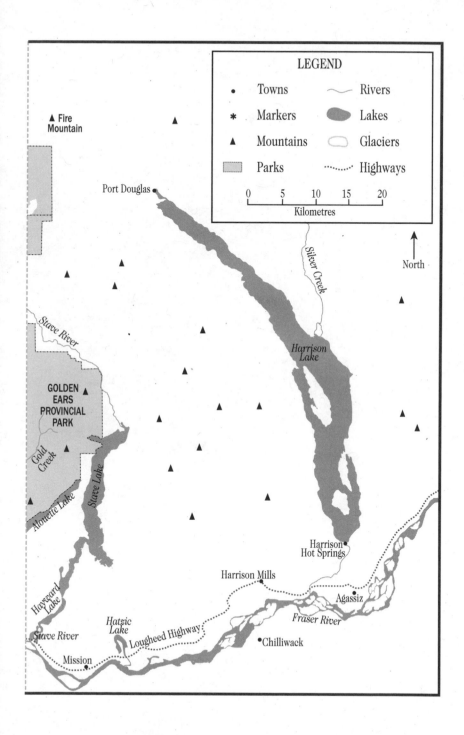

Gold seekers hunker down for the night in glacier country. Traversing glaciers and snow packs is dangerous business, and searchers must be prepared for winter conditions at all times.

Gold Seekers

Over the last 35 years, many rainbow chasers who began their research in the comfort and safety of libraries and their homes decided to take the next step and venture physically into dangerous "Slumach country."

We have carefully reviewed the publications and documentaries that came after our own slim volume of 1972, the first to be written about Slumach's legend. We wanted to know more about these people who staked their reputations on finding Slumach's lost mine, making public their quests and opinions. And we wanted to know what motivated these first-time authors and amateur historians to put themselves at risk.

We do not wish to celebrate, or even mention, those who were cavalier in their searches. We want to focus instead on those who did diligent research, who added to our findings or found things we had missed, or, better yet, came up with information and theories we'd never contemplated.

Understandably, some have created controversy. But by taking risks, they have furthered the truth. And where truth was not available, they have provided careful assumptions, fair analysis and heartfelt (albeit biased) theories about Slumach's legendary gold.

We respectfully call these worthy adventurers "gold seekers," and there are 10 in particular whom we felt merited inclusion for their commitment to the legend's spirit. They ventured along the same, thrilling paths of discovery travelled by Jackson and Volcanic Brown.

This view of Pitt Lake looks south toward the Golden Ears mountains from the head of Pitt Lake.

Don Waite

An RCMP constable finds the last living connection to Slumach

In the late 1960s, Don Waite was a young RCMP constable trained in solving murders, finding missing people and tracking burglars. At 22, the wavy-haired rookie was the youngest detective at the Burnaby, B.C., detachment. He had been designated as "plainclothes," and made privy to the elite investigative minds within the force. He developed skills and a sense of justice that would serve him well in later years as a writer and historian.

After a transfer to the New Westminster detachment, Don assumed new duties at the old courthouse building, the force's base in New Westminster at that time. One day, the corporal-in-charge changed Don's life with a simple request: "I need you to help me move out some case-file boxes from the old vault."

When the corporal unlocked the vault's padlock and flicked the light switch, the single light bulb revealed a circular staircase climbing three levels against walls stacked with dusty files. The room smelled of old paper. As the two police officers entered the high ceiling archives, Waite touched a wooden crate to his right and wondered what purpose this old room had served in the distant past. As they moved boxes around, Waite began to snoop through the files. He pulled out mildewed papers and saw for the first time the handwritten name "Slumach."

Seeing what Waite was holding, the corporal told him, "This is where they hung old Slumach."

"Who?" asked Waite, unfamiliar with the name.

"The Indian. The murderer. January 1891. Put a rope up there, over that beam," said the corporal, pointing high above them.

Waite immediately became intrigued. Even though he later learned that Slumach was in fact hanged not in that room but outside the provincial jail, Waite was launched on a lifelong quest for the truth behind the Slumach story.

Less than a year later, when he had been posted to the small community of Maple Ridge, further out in the Fraser Valley and on the doorstep of Pitt Lake, he began an intense phase in his search for the truth about Slumach after meeting residents of the Katzie Reserve whose handed-down recollections of Slumach's mistreatment under the law were still very much alive. Because of the injustice they felt he had been subjected to, they viewed him almost as a hero.

Constable Waite arrived at the reserve one day as part of his orientation to the area. Seeing a middle-aged Native man carrying two huge fish over his shoulders walking toward him, Waite introduced himself. Chief Joachim Pierre dropped the fish on the ground and extended a scale-coated hand in greeting—the first of many between the two men, and a sign of their early bond of friendship. Trust and mutual respect grew from their honesty with one another. When Joe Pierre and his mother and son died in a tragic car accident in 1971, the six pallbearers were five neighbouring chiefs, and Waite.

It was through Chief Joe Pierre's wife, Agnes, that Waite got to know Pierre's aunt, Amanda Charnley ("Aunt Mandy"). The research on Slumach that Waite had begun among the musty documents in New Westminster's old courthouse and continued over the previous year made his investigative mind want to learn more, and he had heard that Mandy knew the true story, so one day while he was off duty, he met Agnes at the reserve, and together they drove to Mission for a visit.

This first meeting with Aunt Mandy and her husband Clinton was the beginning of Waite's multi-year relationship with the elderly couple, a relationship that was rich in historical anecdotes of First Nations and Whites, Mandy's people, life on the reserve, her deceased father, Peter Pierre (who in 1936 had so clearly interpreted the traditions and beliefs of the Katzie for Dr. Diamond Jenness, an interpretation later published in *The Faith of a Coast Salish Indian*)—and Slumach.

When Waite visited the couple, Clinton would often greet him as he walked up Charnley Street (named after them). They'd sit in the sunlight on the wooden stairs of the only house on the street,

Clinton telling about his young life working from sun-up to sundown in the fields or forests and then tumbling into bed exhausted and falling asleep instantaneously. He had later worked as a butcher, but these days, he said, he relished his retired lifestyle. After his chats with Clinton, Waite would then visit with Mandy and, over the years, the trust between the two continued to grow.

Invited inside their home one day for a special visit, Waite sat across the kitchen table from Aunt Mandy. She smoothed the green vinyl tablecloth, wiped it clean with a wet cloth and poured Agnes

The friendship between Amanda Charnley and Don Waite lasted many years.

and Waite cups of coffee—an attentive and competent host, despite her blindness. (As a young woman, Mandy had been blinded in an accident when she slipped while crossing the frozen Fraser River, falling and bumping her head on the ice.)

Waite had a large notepad before him on the table and his pen at the ready. He smiled, knowing he was about to be let into Aunt Mandy's confidence. She trusted him to retell Slumach's story properly to others. She began:

Here is what my father told me about Slumach, the killing of Louis Bee and the gold that Slumach found in the Pitt country. My father, Peter Pierre, a catechist from the Roman Catholic Order of Mary Immaculate at Mission and medicine man of the Katzie Indian Reserve, was Slumach's nephew.

Father said that Charlie Slumach at the time of the shooting of Bee was closer to 80 than to 60, and that he was a crippled and harmless old widower who lived at the bottom end of Pitt Lake in a shack that was on the abandoned Silver Creek Indian Reserve. He was part Katzie and part Nanaimo Indian. He had a brother named Smum-qua, and a married daughter Mary living at Cowichan on Vancouver Island.

My father spent the last week of Slumach's life with him in prison, teaching him religion and preparing him for the hereafter. It was during that week that Slumach told him what had happened at Alouette Slough. He said that he had been heading up the Lower Pitt River in his canoe to his cabin when he spotted a deer. He shot at the animal from his canoe and then pulled in to the beach to see if he had hit the animal. Seeing blood, he ventured into the bush to look for the wounded animal. After a lengthy and futile search, he was returning to his canoe when he saw two Indians in a canoe out on the water. One was Louis Boulier, a half-French, half-Kanaka, often called Bee for short, and the other was Charlie Seymour, an Indian from Harrison Mills.

Slumach told Peter that Boulier held a grudge against him and, stepping ashore, came at him wielding an axe and shouting, "I'm going to chop your damn head off." Slumach said he raised his shotgun out of sheer fright and fired point blank at Boulier, killing him instantly.

Seymour, the only witness, disappeared into the bush. Slumach placed Boulier's body in the victim's own canoe and set it in midstream to drift down to the fishing party. Slumach did not accompany the body because he feared Boulier's friends might mob him. He then got into his own canoe and paddled upstream to his cabin.

The following day, a boat came out to Slumach's home. The occupants or posse merely fired shots into the house, which resulted in Slumach escaping out the back door and hiding under a fallen tree. The group aboard the boat disgusted Peter by the irresponsible manner in which they carried out their duties. To ensure that Slumach would not return to his home for shelter, they burned it to the ground.

Shown here are Peter Pierre, a Katzie medicine man and Slumach's nephew, and his family. Pierre's daughter Amanda Charnley is in the front row at right. Pierre was with Slumach when he died.

It was to Peter that Slumach eventually surrendered. Peter persuaded his uncle to give himself up to the Indian agent. My father went into the bush after his uncle without a gun, despite warnings from the posse. Peter told them that he was going to see his uncle and not some wild animal. He found Slumach half-starved, hidden under a fallen tree.

According to my father, there was only the hangman, Father Morgan, and himself that actually witnessed the hanging of his uncle, although a great many were present outside the gallows. When the hangman was placing the hood over Slumach's head, the old Indian asked him in Chinook to not waste any time. At that moment, my father closed his eyes and began to pray with Father Morgan. When he opened his eyes all he could see was the dangling rope.

Mandy paused. She was obviously moved by what was to follow. "Slumach was buried in an unknown grave in the prison cemetery in Sapperton, despite attempts by his daughter to get possession of his body to give him a proper burial."

Waite got up to get the coffee pot. The silence settled as he poured Aunt Mandy, Agnes and himself another cup of coffee. He told her how much it meant to him that she was telling him all of this, and assured her that he would treat it with care and portray it word for word.

She thanked him, and then began to tell him about Slumach's gold:

It was during my father's stay in prison that Slumach told him about finding gold in the Pitt country. Slumach told my father that only on one occasion did he ever take gold out of the Pitt. He said that he had met Port Douglas Indians from the head of Harrison Lake coming off Glacier Lake and down Patterson Creek into the Upper Pitt Valley. They told him that they had taken horses partway, but had driven them back towards Port Douglas and had crossed Glacier Lake on foot. They gave him a handful of bullets moulded from gold that they had found in Third Canyon.

Slumach spent the night in the canyon and slept on a bench-shaped rock on the west side of the river. The rock was covered with a rust-coloured moss. When he awoke around 5 a.m., he could scarcely see the sun coming over three mountain peaks for the east wall of the canyon. During this time he was still shrouded in darkness.

As it became lighter, Slumach could see in his own surroundings. Peeling the moss off his rock bed he saw a yellow metal. He dug out some stake nuggets with a penknife and half-filled his shot bag with them. He sold the half-filled bag, which was about the same size of a 10-pound sugar bag, to a storekeeper in New Westminster for $27. The storekeeper went back to England a short time after the purchase.

That, claimed Slumach, was the only gold that he ever took out of the Pitt country. Sitting on the cell bench, Slumach drew a map for Peter of the location where he found the nuggets. Peter memorized the drawing and then destroyed it. Years later he redrew the map. His daughter traced out three copies, however, the original and the copies were destroyed in the 1930s in a house fire.

This version of Slumach's story did not reconcile with the legend and stories that were circulating in the popular journalism of the early 1970s; instead, it rang of truth. Even at this stage of studying records and testimonies, Waite knew that there wasn't any documented reference to Slumach finding a glory hole, let alone one that produced "nuggets as big as hen's eggs." It was increasingly apparent to Waite that such legends about the lost mine of Pitt Lake had begun long after the death of Slumach. At its base, it seemed the legend might be rooted in what he'd just heard.

As Waite puts it in his book, "The accounts did, however, portray the White man's attitude toward Indians and crime by showing the pathetic fashion in which the poor chap, Slumach, got railroaded to the gallows." In Waite's view, newspaper accounts of long ago, by giving a one-sided account of the killing of Bee, sent Slumach to the gallows long before he was even captured.

Don Waite and fellow gold seeker Vic Loffler setting up a camp near Terrarosa Glacier, northeast of Pitt Lake.

Waite had learned that there had been numerous expeditions over the years into the Pitt country to rediscover Slumach's mine, and that they had often met with devastating circumstances. To him, though, an anecdote about the first such expedition may well be what the legend of Slumach's curse is based on.

"Two years after Slumach's death," Waite retells from his notes about that session with Aunt Mandy, "Peter Pierre and Dave Bailey, a half-Scottish, half-Kwikwetlem man, set out for Third Canyon in search of the gold vein that Slumach had described to Peter Pierre. The map scrawled by Slumach in his jail cell was etched in Pierre's mind.

"While attempting to cross a creek on a fallen tree, Pierre lost his footing and took a bad spill, breaking his hip. He had to be carried out. He never went back."

Waite smiles at what may well be the genesis of a fantastic legend. "Aunt Mandy told me her father, Peter Pierre, jokingly suggested that his uncle Slumach 'must have placed a curse on the area.'" Then Waite grows sombre as he recalls that over 30 people have reportedly died in the past 100 years as a result of Slumach's curse.

Don Waite, now 62 and retired from a second career as an aerial photographer, is completing his sixth book, *A Photographic History of North American Gold Hunters.* "Fascination with Slumach led to my writing of books, and sparked my first interest in gold hunters," he says. "We never know where relationships will take us."

Life is like that. So is death. About a year before this edition of *Slumach's Gold* was written, Waite sat in the Simon Pierre Longhouse on the Katzie lands as a roaring fire burned in the rock pit, its smoke rising through a gap in the roof. He listened to the deputy commissioner of the RCMP deliver a eulogy for Agnes Pierre, who had become the Katzie chief years earlier upon the death of her husband, Joe. Many dignitaries attended, and RCMP officers in formal red serge tunics were on hand. Waite and the other pallbearers walked the cedar coffin around the lodge two times, and then to a waiting hearse. Later, standing at the cemetery in swirling snow, Waite eased the rope through his hands as he helped lower his friend's casket into the ground.

The funeral marked the passing of the last of three influential people in Waite's search for the truth about Slumach. Chief Joachim Pierre, Aunt Mandy and Agnes Pierre, who had been the closest living links to the real Slumach, had each nudged history in a more credible direction.

A broken shovel leans against a derelict cabin. Such cabins were common throughout British Columbia, humble lodgings for gold seekers who dreamed of richer abodes.

Jon Ferry

A journalist hikes the high country in his search for the mine

In 1983, Vancouver television station CKVU and *The Province* sent a television news crew of three, plus a newspaper reporter and photographer, into the bush to search for Slumach's gold, taking along a guide and a dowser to help them. Was it a publicity stunt, or a genuine undertaking?

Both media outlets launched a concurrent series of stories in October that year, smack in the middle of the broadcast ratings season. On October 9, *The Province* sported the headline "Gold Fever! Looking for the Lost Creek Mine." Reporter Jon Ferry engaged his readers with his telling of Slumach's story and his intrepid team's plan to unearth the glory hole.

Each morning for a week, Ferry told the story of their search in the paper's early edition and, each evening, television reporter Dale Robins gave viewers of CKVU's *First News* a visual account. Each story recounted their late September wanderings up richly forested mountains and down rock-strewn valleys and into the Widgeon Lake area at the southwest corner of Pitt Lake, long rumoured to be the secret location of Slumach's lost hoard. Experienced Abbotsford prospector Gary McIsaac guided the team as they searched for minerals, using his dowsing skills to detect gold. His task was to show the way to the multi-million-dollar find.

McIsaac had had a vision of Slumach standing in the mine, and it had driven him toward this location. Curses be damned! They were on their way. Two days in, the team reported making camp "nestled beside a lake of jade and sheltered by sheer cliffs." McIsaac broke out the tool of his trade: a "dowsing bug" that contained a canister of gold and mercury. It started "to bounce around wildly." The next day's report saw the team suffering "sheer exhaustion" but, undaunted, they scaled a "ladder of boulders" to a ridge leading toward Widgeon Peak.

Gold seekers cross rushing water at Widgeon Creek in Slumach country. Rough water tumbles down dozens of creeks and rivers in this area.

"It's a throat-stopping sight. We are in the land of the gods. In the heavens ahead are the parapets of a celestial castle," Ferry wrote, referring to the surrounding peaks that created an enthralling vista. Below, they could see a "circle of huge boulders" at the bottom of a valley, where McIsaac believed the mine might be found.

The "valley of the rocks," as they dubbed it, proved to be impossible to reach. McIsaac's dowsing bug was working overtime, but an 800-foot cliff with no visible route down was their undoing. Equipment and people were wearing out and, for their own safety, they backed off their quest.

Their recounting cited the "thrills and perils of this dangerous mountain country," and the team vowed to return for a second expedition. However, Ferry said in a 2007 interview that he knows of no team members who ever actually went back in search of Slumach's elusive mine, or of any who have died from the curse. He summed up the trip by saying, "It was rather magical up there."

Yet the question remains: What lies beneath the circle of rocks?

Norm

He claimed they found the tent-shaped rock—and had pictures to prove it

"You wrote that Slumach book, didn't you?"

The friendly, silver-bearded fellow who posed that question sat on a community group's board of directors in Mission, B.C., with author Brian Antonson. As talk got around to other parts of their lives, he connected Brian's name with our 1972 publication. Norm (not his real name) had pored over his copy of the book many times.

Over several meetings, Norm and Brian talked at length about the legend and the glory hole rumoured to be hidden among the peaks northeast of Pitt Lake. "Do you think there's really gold up there?" Norm asked.

"Well, if there *is* gold in the story, that's where I think it'll be found," said Brian.

Norm then offered up a tantalizing tidbit. "A few of us know a helicopter pilot who flies a postal worker into the Stave Glacier area every year. He picks him up a couple of weeks later, and his packsack is loaded with gold. He hasn't heard from him for a couple of years and thinks he may be dead." Norm paused before continuing. "So, if the pilot doesn't hear from the prospector this year, he's going to take *us* in there!"

Norm studied Brian's expression to see how this was going over before continuing. "We think it's Slumach's mine."

We had heard versions of this story before. After we'd published our book in 1972, we had each received calls from people who claimed to have been at the mine, or to know precisely where it was located. All had been willing to share some knowledge, but not everything they knew.

Norm winked and said, "I'll let you know if we find anything."

Some months later, in 1985, the community group's board of directors met at Norm's home. While others were drinking coffee during a break, Norm motioned Brian to follow him into a back room.

There, Norm handed the surprised Brian a sheaf of photographs. Brian looked at the top one. "The tent-shaped rock!" he burst out.

Norm smiled and nodded.

"Where did you get this shot?"

Norm grinned widely. "I took it."

Now, anyone who knows the stories about Slumach's lost gold knows that a key feature of the mine's location is a tent-shaped rock.

This dramatic view of Mamquam Glacier in Garibaldi Provincial Park shows the forbidding country around Pitt Lake, where many say there is gold to be found. Above the treeline, rocks, snowfields and glaciers, conditions are even more treacherous.

Jackson's letter was the first to describe this: "I buried part of the gold at the foot of a large tent-shaped rock, facing the creek. You can't miss it. There is a mark cut out in it." Others who claim to have found the mine have identified this rock, and countless prospectors have imagined its appearance.

What Brian saw in Norm's photographs fit our imaginings to the proverbial T. The rock was roughly pyramidal in shape, like an old miner's tent. Near the top of it, a chunk was missing as if it had been "cut out." It stood in the open, the ground around it covered in moss. In fact, it looked very much like the artist's concept-drawing of the site we used in the 1972 book.

Brian leafed through the half-inch stack of photos. In some, two people were standing near the rock, so it could be estimated at about 10 feet high. Norm had taken numerous pictures of the site from all angles, and of his partners as they stood in the middle of what they believed to be Jackson's find.

"And—did you find gold?"

Norm smiled again. "We dug through a foot of moss at the base of the rock and found nuggets. We brought them out. They're gold, alright."

So there it was: many years after we'd first looked into the legend and found the reference to the tent-shaped rock, Brian was holding pictures of it, talking with a man who claimed to have taken raw gold from the site.

Brian never saw Norm again. He died a while later—not a victim of the mine's supposed curse, but of a lifetime of smoking—and the secret of this mine's location went with him to his grave. But we want to believe that he and his partners had found gold, somewhere in the high mountains near the Stave Glacier, and he had chosen to share just a bit of his secret!

Jack Mould

He lives on the edge—of life and of the mine

Jack Mould and the Curse of Gold—The Slumach Legend Lives On.
The rhyming title of Elizabeth Hawkins' 1993 book leaps from
a cover festooned with skulls, a hangman's noose and glittering
chunks of raw gold. And between the covers lies a romp—a rol-
licking tale about a loveable rogue and his lifelong quest for
Slumach's gold.

One might wonder if the gold Jack Mould has sought lo these
many years is indeed at all connected with Slumach, for Mould has
focussed his search right where his father told him to, at the headwaters of Bute Inlet, but far to the northwest of the traditional search
area for seekers of Slumach's hoard.

That said, Slumach's story weaves in and out of Mould's. Hawkins
calls him "larger than life," and his story would appear to be just
that. In a life replete with stints in prison, toiling in logging camps,
unlucky love (and lots of it!), the tragedy of families torn apart,
sabotage, attempted suicide and a constant feeling of "What could
possibly happen next?" Jack's unwavering focus has been to find the
legendary glory hole guarded by Slumach's curse.

The Spanish were the first to explore this part of British
Columbia's coast, and Jack and his father found evidence of their
workings high in the mountains at the head of Bute Inlet. Did the
Spaniards take gold from this part of the mainland? Did they leave
any behind? Have others—perhaps Slumach—found it since? This is
the meat of Jack's Slumach search.

Mould's father, Charlie, searched the inlet in vain for gold, but
he found plenty of evidence that others had been there before him.
An old carved cedar door, bearing images of Spanish soldiers, stood
as mute evidence of their presence here. Had Spaniards carved the
door? Was it perhaps the Coast Salish people who had encountered
them as they moved along the fjords, nudging their boats in near
shore, slipping into the wooded hillsides in search of any treasures

This view looks down from the high country onto the upper Pitt River, seen here winding through steep and dangerous terrain.

the land might have to offer? Whatever its origin, the door was there and Jack saw it. Then there was the iron bucket and the pulley block and tackle rig. Other evidence spoke volumes to the young Mould as he learned at his father's side to thirst for this elusive shiny metal and the promise of incredible fortune.

What would any story of Slumach's gold be without its own tent-shaped rock? Jackson's original description of his find has fuelled imaginations for over a century, and Mould's story locates it high in the snows of the Bute Inlet area. It looks down over the Inlet from its perch, or rather, *did*: a photo taken in the 1990s shows Jack with the rock at his home. The object in the photo looks more like a climber's cairn than a rock shaped like a tent. It's tall and slim, and sits atop a collection of other roughly hewn rocks of similar shape. The actual rock is perhaps three feet tall at maximum and doesn't convey the image of a tent, but it's Jack's version, and it fits with his story.

Mould also brought a dowser into his search. He didn't find any precious metal, but he did discover bones in the high country, bones that proved to be those of a male and a young girl. He speculates as to whose bones they might be: one of the young women Slumach lured into the bush? Volcanic Brown? Another hapless gold seeker? Or are these much older Spanish bones? The answers have proved as elusive as the lost treasure.

Mould hasn't found gold. Although he doesn't want to believe in Slumach's curse, his life has taken many untoward turns, and his attempts to find the hidden trove have been thwarted by disaster, weather and mishaps of his own or others' making. He did admit to video producer Michael Collier in the early 1990s that "definitely I stronger and stronger believe there had to be a curse." [*sic*] For Jack Mould, the secret of Slumach still lies hidden in the forbidding mountains of Bute Inlet, in spite of his lifetime of searching.

Donna

She claims they found the mine—but the gold was gone

What if someone actually found Slumach's mine, but the gold was already gone? That's what an Alberta farmer named Donna (who preferred that her last name not be published) claims to have discovered in 1994.

Readers of the October 10, 1995, edition of the *Vancouver Sun* sat down to a lengthy article by reporter Mark Hume that detailed the legendary Slumach mine story, reminding the knowledgeable and luring the novice. It profiled the earliest gold seekers, like Jackson and Volcanic Brown, who may have found it.

Donna and her husband studied aerial photographs of the Pitt Lake region and, using Jackson's letter as a guide, searched for a valley that matched his description. In the end, she told the *Sun* "we were able to determine there was only one place it could be. I guess you might call it a detective job." Jackson's clues, including a description of the hidden valley, the white colour of the creek's water, no visible entrance or exit to the creek, and the tent-shaped rock, all pointed Donna to one valley that was north beyond the head of Pitt Lake.

Their first backpacking trip into the wild country of Garibaldi Provincial Park proved too much for the couple, so they returned a year later, using a helicopter to deliver them to their search area. And sure enough, they found the tent-shaped rock and the creek running with whitewater, but with no visible entrance or exit to the valley. They had found what they believed to be the location of Slumach's legendary hoard.

What they found next brought their search to a rapid and disappointing halt: the site was riddled with deep pits and tailings, the obvious leave-behinds of a small mining operation. Someone had been in to the site with heavy machinery, likely a backhoe brought in by helicopter. Whoever had been there had dug the pits, left the tailings where they fell and departed. If there ever *was* gold in this hidden valley, there was none left for Donna.

A gold seeker heads into the mist, hoping his fortune lies ahead on the Slumach trail.

Michael Collier

Hollywood North tackles the lost mine tale

Any way you look at it, the Slumach story is an alloy at best—part truth and part fiction. And that justifies the wonderful juxtaposition of fact and fancy that is the docudrama *Curse of the Lost Gold Mine.*

The expedition leader is Michael Collier, who spent 15 years researching the prospects of gold near Pitt Lake before appending his near-two-week exploration of the area in 1994 to a theatrical retelling of the legend that he himself produced for television. The now-retired Collier told us in 2007 that "as a kid, living on Pitt River Road in Coquitlam during the 1950s, our family bought produce from an old farmer, and it was he who told my parents about Slumach and the lost gold mine. I stood nearby, absolutely enthralled—a kid no higher than the farmer's tabletop."

It was a motivation that would never leave him. He had told us he had read our book *In Search of a Legend* and Don Waite's *Kwant'stan* in the early 1970s. He got hooked, and began his own research. Eventually, he built a cabin on Pitt Lake, spending family vacations there and exploring the area. "I always kept an eye out for the tent-shaped rock," he says. Over the years Collier has canoed much of Pitt Lake, and refers to it as "big and wild." Having climbed many of the region's mountain peaks, he says that the lost gold mine "could be right there in front of you, but you'd never know it."

Three decades ago, as a young filmmaker, Collier began a documentary about the lost mine, and filmed his own first expedition into the area. "We were young and inexperienced—both as gold seekers and as business people. I wasn't able to raise the financing necessary to complete that Slumach project." At that time—and this serves history well—he filmed an interview with Amanda Charnley (Aunt Mandy), preserving important parts of the Slumach story she'd first disclosed to Waite. He kept the rights to this footage for use in the documentary he would eventually make.

Gold seekers traverse one of the many snowfields and glaciers blanketing the area and possibly concealing Volcanic Brown's last camp.

Does he believe Slumach had gold? "I'm skeptical," he says today. Then he smiles and recalls, "But Amanda Charnley said Slumach had gold, and that couldn't help but fan the flames … "

By the 1990s Collier was an established filmmaker with proven credentials, and he was able to secure funding for his long-dreamed-of film based on the legend of the Pitt Lake mine. This allowed him to devote himself full time to his research, which included many days spent at newspaper archives, museums and libraries around British Columbia. He also sought out old-timers, in addition to present-day gold seekers.

This thoroughness extends to how they set up the film's story. Early on in the film, the exploration team is shown in the New Westminster Public Library, going over old newspaper accounts and assorted documents. They describe their approach: they will hike into a specific area and try to locate Volcanic Brown's last camp. Their premise? If gold was found in the camp and Brown had indeed found a motherlode, then somewhere within half a day's walk should be evidence of a mine or workings.

Collier's storytelling encourages more future gold seekers than it dissuades. The film weaves together two stories: one from a distant past full of myth and legend, as told by actor Donnelly Rhodes, the other chronicling a present-day expedition led by Collier. Historical footage and current interviews round out this docudrama.

Donnelly Rhodes plays an irascible character, a pipe-smoking pioneer at home in a log cabin, where he is seated in front of a river-rock fireplace. As the kindling sparks, he looks to the viewer and promises, "I'm going to tell you a story … only thing I will ask of you— don't ask me to say it's true. You know how stories go … " He puffs thoughtfully on his briar pipe and winks mischievously. Then the re-enactment of Slumach's murder of Louis Bee begins—on sepia-toned film evocative of the early days of cinematography. The soundtrack features Native chanting.

Slumach is shown as a long-grey-haired 50-year-old. He encounters Bee, who is seen getting out of a canoe, almost immediately. Slumach is quick to murder him, though in later replays of the scene, as telling details (which the reader knows well) evolve, other versions of the Slumach-Bee encounter are also re-enacted. Bee's threatening and Slumach's hiding are portrayed to balance the story. Eventually Bee is seen as a provocateur carrying a "one-bit axe" and yelling to Slumach, "I'm coming up there to chop your head off."

Rhodes' pioneer/prospector, sporting a scruffy beard and peering over the top of his glasses, leans back in his chair before goading the viewer: "So, if you're thinking of taking off half-cocked into Slumach country, there's something you should know." He then starts to talk about the curse, building on the legend. In gravelly tones, he tells about the murders of various women (three Whites, five Indian), focussing particularly on Molly Tynan, whom he says was a waitress at the Sasquatch Cafe and who, when found, had "Slumach's knife buried deep into her heart." He recounts the disappearance of other ne'er-do-wells who followed Slumach in hopes of stealing his gold. They faced "deadly hardships," and always got

Veteran actor Donnelly Rhodes plays the old prospector in Michael Collier's mid-1990s docudrama *Curse of the Lost Gold Mine*.

lost when Slumach disappeared "as if he dropped through a tear in the universe."

As Rhodes' character tends the fire to help dry his wool socks hanging in the background, he talks of "expedition after expedition," and the docudrama is soon following Michael Collier's team of three adventurers, one of whom is a mountain guide. Their 11-day trek, starting with a helicopter drop-off, enables them to follow, after a fashion, the last route of Volcanic Brown and that of his subsequent search party. As they venture into menacingly foggy milieus, Rhodes' voice reminds the viewer: "There's still danger in Slumach country."

The hikers spend much of their 45-mile exploration hypothesizing about "ol' Slumach." They flash newspaper clippings that show headlines from the *Daily Province* (later *The Province*) of lost-mine stories from 1906, 1910, 1939, 1951, 1953, 1964, 1971, 1974, 1983 and 1989, each one either claiming there were more victims or reporting on searches.

The sharing of fresh insights is left mostly to Rhodes' character, who looks convincingly authentic in his long-sleeved shirt and vest,

Members of Michael Collier's team take five during their quest for gold.

loose tie and with a tendency to peer across the top of a kerosene lantern when he's got a point to make. "No witnesses for defence were called," he says of the trial. And "Slumach was never asked to tell his side of the story." He goes on to claim that Slumach "even 'wept a bit' as his trial progressed."

Noting emphatically (in fact, all of this character's observations are delivered *very* emphatically) that "gold fever was an epidemic at the turn of the century," Rhodes' pioneer/prospector offers his take on the motivation behind all the searches for Slumach's lost mine: "It's greed [that] describes the never-ending tale of human tragedy—natural-born greed. Well, that's as good as a curse any old day of the week."

In the mix of recreated scenes, modern searchers and the pioneer's storytelling, various elements come to light, most of them of questionable accuracy:

- the report that on the day of Slumach's hanging, a woman appeared with a canoe full of gold to pay for Slumach's release;
- the suggestion that Justice Drake, who sentenced Slumach to hang, offered to commute his sentence to life imprisonment if he divulged the source of his gold;
- the literal translation of "Nika memloose, mine memloose" to mean "the mine dies with me";
- the reference to *John* Jackson, which, interestingly, is the name we used—mistakenly, we believe—in our 1972 book; Jackson's letter was, in fact, signed "W. Jackson"; and
- the claim that Jackson dispatched a companion, which is a new twist to the Jackson tale.

Surprisingly, this docudrama has Slumach passing his secret on to a son, who reportedly took a helper along to search for his father's mine. Since the film claims that only the helper returned, it seems to suggest Slumach's "own son" was the first victim of the curse.

Intertwined with the hikers' mist-shrouded climb through the difficult terrain is the story of how Volcanic Brown sensed he was being followed on one journey into Stave Glacier, then turned back to find his stalker dead, having fallen over a cliff—another hapless victim of the curse.

Partway into their exploration across the mountains, the search team finds the remains of a campsite at an elevation of 6,000 feet and sets about determining if it might have been Brown's. Collier remembers that as they dug below the moss, they found old, charred wood from a campfire, "left as though a marker." They found something else as well. Partially hidden under the lip of a large boulder was an old crucible that must have been there for nearly 80 years. This type of strong, metal canister, later authenticated by mining experts, was used around Brown's time by experienced prospectors. Collier told us, "Only sophisticated prospectors of those days would have carried one of these. They'd use it to grind at the quartz to loosen the mix of gold and start the separation process." It could not be confirmed as Brown's, but it was a "very, very old indicator" that at least one serious gold prospector camped at the head of Stave Glacier around that period. If it wasn't Brown, Collier asks, "Who else?"

"At that elevation, winter can come in quickly," Collier told us. He said that Brown, after being caught in a storm, nearly died from the perilous temperatures and that, having cut off his toes to save himself from further frostbite damage, he put a tin can over the end of his foot so he could hike out more easily.

The members of Collier's expedition are well equipped, professionally guided and comforted by having radio contact with the outside world. Even so, when they move on from what they believe is Brown's last camp to go further into the Stave Glacier area, they become trapped in a terrible, sudden snowstorm that nearly rips their tents from their pegs and strands them on the mountainside for three days. It was as though Slumach's curse, long blamed for nasty winds, was about to end their quest in disaster. Collier remembers this vividly: "The whole tent was trying to be airborne. We were lying inside it, just trying to hold it down. Death was very close."

At the end of the docudrama, Rhodes' character reappears, resting near the warmth of the fire in his log cabin and offering a final warning to those who would be "lacing up your boots, picking up a shovel and a map and heading for these hills." He admonishes, "They say that Slumach guards the entrance to his mine to this very day."

Collier's gold seekers set up camp in glacier country.

Curse of the Lost Gold Mine was broadcast Canada-wide on the Canwest Global Network. Winning silver awards at both the New York Film Festival and the Charleston Worldfest International Film Festival, the docudrama brought the Slumach story international recognition. Collier says that he continues to get requests for DVD copies of the production from across North America and Europe: "Whether these are from armchair enthusiasts for Slumach's legend or eventual gold seekers who may one day find something remains to be seen!"

Daryl Friesen

His teenage commitment to find the mine becomes a lifelong quest

Daryl Friesen's 1984 excursion with his dad to an abandoned silver mine in the hills near Yale, B.C., sparked a lifetime passion for treasure hunting in the 12-year-old.

Enamoured of the thrill of the chase and inspired by a local library file about lost mines, the curious boy began a relentless, lifelong search for Slumach's gold.

As a teenager in Langley, B.C., bored with high school and fast-food delivery jobs, Friesen and his teenaged friends acted on their dreams to pursue outdoor adventure and excitement. The lure of Slumach's gold provided an incentive.

Friesen's e-book, *Seekers of Gold*, chronicles his tenacious search for the mine between 1984 and 1991. His father supported his son's quest with encouragement and frequent trips up Pitt Lake in the family boat.

"My dad … was the one person I thought believed in me, because when I was young, he took me up to that lake and up to those mountains and he made me believe that the gold was there. He made me believe I could search for it, and anything was possible."

On one of his first trips, Friesen met an elderly First Nations man known as Houseboat Harry, who told him that there was no gold in the upper Pitt region; rather, it was behind the head of DeBeck Creek. Pumped up with anticipation, Friesen became consumed with the search, especially after he received an anonymous envelope containing a map with an X marking the mine's location, and barely legible notes on the side.

Friesen was also mesmerized by an audiotape made in 1969 and given to him by a Mrs. Smittberg, who owned a cabin on the shore of Pitt Lake, right next to the mouth of DeBeck Creek. On the tape she talked about a group of prospectors who, in her absence, had broken into the cabin to find shelter after their boat sank in Pitt

This aerial view of Slumach country gives another perspective on the treacherous country north of Pitt Lake. Did Jackson and Volcanic Brown explore these many creeks? Did they find gold?

Lake. They had left a map in the cabin marked with an X on top of a small canyon (later identified as Spindle Canyon) just north of Widgeon Lake.

Fuelled by the wonderful energy, enthusiasm and reckless perseverance associated with youth, Friesen and his buddies explored, hiked, camped, tramped, helicoptered, sea-planed, drove, crawled and otherwise blitzed their way around every boulder, canyon, stream and river in the upper Pitt Lake and Garibaldi Provincial Park areas. He describes in his book how nerves became frayed after one soaking-wet hike up DeBeck Creek that involved tripping, falling, and pushing through treacherous terrain. But even unpredictable weather, steep slopes, flat tires and prickly devil's club couldn't squelch Friesen's unflappable spirit. Like gold-smitten prospectors 150 years ago, Friesen was dedicated to finding his strike.

Still, the threat of Slumach's curse seems to lurk in Friesen's book: "Once you would get close to where you wanted to be, some weather factor would always get in your way and crush your plans. It really makes you wonder if what they say about a curse on this place is true."

Sometimes Friesen and his prospecting partner, Shawn Gryba, seemed to come deliciously close to the gold. During one backbreaking day of panning in Spindle Canyon, success appeared to be at hand:

> I couldn't believe what I saw resting within the black sand at the bottom of my gold pan. I was not seeing things; I was staring at one very small piece of gold about the size of the end of my fingernail. I screamed in ecstasy as I brought it out of the water and into the light of day. Here was truly a sign there may be something in this canyon after all.

In 2007, however, Friesen admitted the sample was simply too insignificant to get assayed.

Eventually, Friesen's driven search for treasure compelled him to link up with an older generation of gold seekers who embraced the legend; Mike Boileau was one. (Once, while searching for Slumach's gold in Spindle Canyon, Boileau had come across the wreckage of a Mitchell B-25 bomber that had crashed north of Widgeon Lake in 1953, just above the lip of upper Spindle Canyon. Rumours said it went down with gold aboard, but none was ever found.)

Friesen also met Bill Cull, a prospector from Maple Ridge, who claimed to have found a tent-shaped rock with the initial J carved at the bottom, supposedly in the upper Stave area. Friesen believes the J stands for Jackson.

Intrigued by Don Waite's writings, Friesen interviewed another seeker, Stuart Brown, who claimed to have found the mine in Garibaldi Provincial Park in 1971. Their visit occurred in 2000, three years before Brown died.

Friesen began politely, yet curiously, asking, "When was the last time you went up there?" Brown told him it had been in 1980. Then came the real question.

"Did you ever find gold?"

Brown's casual response, "Yeah," was frustratingly short.

"How much?"

"Considerable," he replied, continuing the evasion.

Friesen tried another approach. "Would you ever talk to anyone about where you went?"

"I am a little leery about it all. I'd not go back at my age. And to tell about it would be endangering people's lives. No one in their right mind would ever go in there with that terrain."

Friesen pressed for details: "Is it anywhere near Stave Glacier?"

"Well, that's a matter of distance. But I can say it is generally east of Stave Glacier, near Terrarosa Glacier."

"I guess you would not be able to show the area on a map would you?"

"You have to know the country … "

When Friesen told Brown that Brown was the only person still alive who was on record as claiming to know where the mine was, Brown said that another person had gone with him once, but not all the way. He also said that the mine could be reached through a circuitous route that included Fire Lake, but then added, "I don't think there is much use in me discussing this. What good would it do? I am only endangering your life."

"Is it closer to the upper Pitt or the upper Stave?"

"Offhand, I would say Stave," said Brown, ending the conversation.

Speculation about Stuart Brown's motives has permeated Friesen's views on the legend. He believes Brown's assertions to be true: that there is gold in Garibaldi Provincial Park, and that Brown genuinely

Gold seekers triangulate with a topographical map, deciding which route will lead to the high country and perhaps gold.

wanted to stake a claim. Always compelled to follow up on new leads, Friesen and some friends trekked into the furthest reaches of Garibaldi. Instead of finding gold, they found themselves fending off two cougars.

The entrance to an old mine shaft at lake level frames gold seekers and a view of the high country where gold may lie.

Friesen devotes an entire chapter of *Seekers of Gold* to out-lawed prospecting in Garibaldi Provincial Park (the southern half of which was renamed Golden Ears Provincial Park in 1960). He speculates that the reason the provincial government banned prospecting in all provincial parks in 1965 was because they knew there was gold in the Garibaldi area and wanted to protect it. Friesen claims that rumours along this line abound, including this intriguing tidbit: "There are also stories of guard towers built near Remote Peak, which are used by agents of the government to protect the gold canyon. The towers were built by the government during World War II to watch for attacks by the Japanese, and have since been taken up to watch for prospectors going into the area during the right time of year when the gold reveals itself." (The presence of gold in Garibaldi was verified in 1965 by a former geologist with the Geological Survey of Canada.) Friesen also discusses in this chapter various Americans who may have found gold in the area and mined it—outside the law, of course.

In 2002 Langley businessman and pilot Dean Russell asked Friesen to accompany him up to Pitt Lake in his Robinson R44 helicopter. It was a sunny August day when they took off from Langley; Russell hoped that Friesen could pinpoint the Mitchell B-25 crash and identify possible mine sites. Their mission was thwarted when a tremendous gust of wind forced the chopper to crash and slide down a steep, icy precipice. Only a rocky outcropping held them back from a horrendous descent into Pitt Lake. Fortunately, no one was hurt. "No doubt this was Slumach's warning to 'stay back,'" quips Friesen.

Today, at 35, Friesen no longer speeds dangerously around Langley like he did when he was 19, high on solving the Slumach legend. But he's still driven. In addition to managing his company, Spindle Explorations, Friesen looks forward to completing a historical fiction book about a real-life British Columbia prospector, Johnny Chance. And he is almost finished *Seekers of Gold, Part II*, which details his 2002 helicopter crash, and presents clues to possible gold locations inside Garibaldi Provincial Park, where Friesen continues to believe Slumach's mine is located.

When asked if he'll continue to search for Slumach's gold, Friesen's answer reflects a more mature, but no less subdued determination. "What's the truth? That's what I want to find," he concludes. "It's possible that the Browns, Slumach and Jackson all found gold, but in different locations."

Sylvio Heufelder

Television tells the tale on an international scale

A German television show produced and directed by Sylvio Heufelder merits gold-seeker status because it launched a search in the early 1990s that gained an international audience for the legend.

"The Mystery of Old Slumach" was created as an episode of the German *Treasure Hunters* series. The production crew's research led them initially to Archie Miller, the former curator at Irving House Historical Centre (now the New Westminster Museum and Archives), who tantalizes the viewer with the line "there are people who say they've found it." And then the crew goes off, searching for the motherlode.

A local guide leads them up Pitt Lake via canoe and on foot into the lush woodlands surrounding the lake. In fine August weather, they follow well-established trails, discovering crumbling miners' shacks, quartz veins, hot springs and creeks rich in spawning fish. Along the way they encounter a local resident, who reports that Slumach's relatives had talked about the old man having a nugget the size of his hand—more fuel for the gold seeker's fire!

The story weaves in Volcanic Brown's search as the one having the most credibility, given Brown's well-earned fame and the widely publicized searches for him when he disappeared. They seek what might have been his route but, several days in, they realize that Brown's find was likely much higher up the mountain than the location they had reached. They decide to take a helicopter into the high ground above 6,000 feet, where his last camp was found. Despite a thorough reconnaissance of this high country, they find no trace of Brown's camp. (After almost 115 years, one doesn't wonder that it would be gone.) Their helicopter search for Jackson's valley bearing a stream with no beginning or end and a tent-shaped rock also proves futile.

After this, the film shows an interview with well-known British Columbia historian and politician Bill Barlee, who lends credibility to the program. He talks of Jackson's letter: "The original letter was date-stamped from a government office ... I examined it very closely ... it uses certain phrases only used in the 1880s and 1890s." He notes further that "it's not like other letters ... this is a genuine letter ... and the terminology makes it genuine and the date stamp makes it more genuine." For a historian of Barlee's stature to judge the

In the 1880s Slumach lived in a cabin next to Widgeon Slough (seen here in the lower left corner of the photo) at the south end of Pitt Lake.

letter credible adds tremendous weight to it. Barlee claims, "There's no doubt Slumach had something to do with it."

Archie Miller sums up the show: "There are a number of extra stories … but it all comes back to this thing that the … legend grows, but there was this man, he did something bad, he paid the penalty, and he was finding gold. I think it exists … we just haven't found it yet."

An interesting footnote to this show emerged in discussions with Slumach historian Don Waite. In 1987 one of the show's researchers contacted Waite a few months before the documentary makers arrived in B.C. By this time, Waite had a very impressive collection of archival notes on Slumach, including his own journals from trips to the headwaters of the upper Pitt River and a 1986 trip into Fire Lake with a man who declared he'd found gold near Terrarosa Glacier. Waite agreed to the researcher's request to photocopy all his Slumach files and have them bound into book form.

Well-known British Columbia prospector Volcanic Brown disappeared in 1931 while searching for Slumach's mine. Eleven ounces of raw gold found in his last camp added to the speculation that he may have discovered it … was it Jackson's find that he stumbled upon?

Waite met the researcher in Vancouver a week or two later to give him the book. When the German film crew was preparing for their trip, they contacted Waite and asked if he'd be the intermediary between the crew and the Katzie elders in order to set up a meeting with them. Waite chaired a meeting with the elders, who came to the consensus that they did not want to be visited by the crew. They seemed to object to an apparent White appropriation of Indian history. "They tramp through our cemetery," they said to Waite. "All they want is the story, and we never seem to get anything in return."

Waite faxed this information back to Germany, but the film crew came over anyway. They visited Waite's home and asked him to serve as historian for their project. Waite agreed to a filmed interview, believing it was important to ensure the stories were recorded as well as passed along orally and that this was done with the approval of the elders. However, because the crew did not obtain permission from the Katzie, Waite refused to allow his footage to be used and the filmmakers interviewed historian Bill Barlee instead.

John Lovelace

An aviator flies into the site in a new search

In 2002 a production crew working for *Wings Over Canada*, a popular television show with a good reputation for its reporting on history and geography, ventured into the Coast Mountains and onto the windswept waters of Pitt Lake. Flying a bush plane over log booms beneath mist-shrouded mountains, the crew landed at the head of Pitt Lake, where the upper Pitt River flows into it. They were determined to at least find some fun behind the Slumach legend, if not gold.

In the resulting documentary, John Lovelace, pilot-adventurer, avid historian and the show's host for the episode "Lost Gold Mine of Pitt Lake," tells viewers he wants to get to the heart of Slumach's story. He says he is perplexed that no one has discovered the lost treasure, since the area it's supposed to be in is only 15 air miles out of Vancouver.

Some of the episode's shortcomings become evident early on when the storytellers inform us that Slumach was the only man to be hanged in New Westminster—which, of course, is not true. We are shown the Westminster Hotel and told it was built in Slumach's time, even though its sign clearly reads "Est. 1898" and we know that he was hanged in 1891. And they say that "Boulbie" is Louis Bee's last name, not the usual "Boulier." In spite of these discrepancies, the story they tell is enjoyable and exciting, and features some unlikely findings.

Mining engineer Tom Morrison serves as their guide, and says that here they'll find copper, nickel and maybe gold. But he sets the crew on alert right from the start when he advises, "Gold will make a fool of you, every time." Having met his share of gold seekers and knowing the history of prospecting, Morrison is familiar with the haphazard thinking that leads people astray in search of gold. ("In these mountains, that could get you killed," he says). Morrison says "you can take at face value" that gold exists around here and that,

Upper Pitt River joins the lake in a broad delta, while fabled Corbold Creek joins the Pitt from the east, near Alvin. Gold seekers often take this route into the high country, where they believe Jackson and Brown found their fortunes.

given the extent of mining in the 1880s, most of the creeks in this area would have been searched. That some gold made it through here is history, he says, and he believes that persistent rumours of it continuing to be found suggest "the stuff has to come from somewhere."

The show goes on to describe Slumach as a "wily miner … adept at hiding his mine." One "old-timer," it says, claims that Jackson's gold looked like it came from bedrock, and while there *is* lots of bedrock about, it is covered by overgrowth and protected by thick bushes that block out sunlight, causing heavy moss growth that reduces visibility. And, at best, such places are often located in streams that are "here one year, and gone the next."

Other factors make the mine hard to find, but the lack of a map is not one of them, Morrison asserts. "I could draw you a sketch map of these mountains, and you'd never follow it. The country is too big."

He continues to describe the surroundings as the camera pans around. From beautiful shots of huge timbers fallen over creeks and gushing waterfalls cascading into rocky caverns, one gets the impression that these creek beds are filled with water much of the year and certainly too dangerous to approach. Rushing streams twist back on themselves, and some of these waterways act like "nature's sluice" according to the narrator. Gold panners work hard to separate gold from gravel, often running water over the rocks, yet here it happens naturally as the rough waters twirl and grind the stones. This forcefulness calms eventually, opening up new areas for prospectors to kneel and ply their trade. Indeed, because "all the good ground has been panned over and panned over," it is *only* when rough water carves new routes for creeks and opens up new gravel beds that fresh opportunities arise. That must happen with some regularity, we must surmise, since we're told this is where "prospectors come in all the time."

Because the region is accessible only by boat or seaplane, the adventurers hike where there are no roads. Both sides of this river once had homesteaders, but they gave up and moved on long ago. Now there are only ruins and remnants of old logging roads, evidence of broken dreams.

The film crew does find one local resident, however, a fisherman living in a cabin who confidently claims that Jackson "climbed up the highest point" in this area and it was from there that he spotted gold in a stream below. But, he says, "streams disappear," referring to the constant changes in the landscape caused by fluctuating weather conditions and shifting water levels, changes that have made following Jackson's lead such a challenge to would-be gold seekers. Despite these impediments, Jackson is said to have invited an American friend to meet him in New Westminster, where he told him, "Jock, keep looking. It's there beyond your wildest dreams."

Lovelace, Morrison and the film crew eventually come upon the Geraks, who built and own the Pitt Lake Resort. They set out together to find a particular creek in what Dan Gerak calls "the hidden valley."

On the way there, the excitement is palpable when the pilot and his crew see a stream roiling through bedrock and just out of reach. They speculate that this is exactly the type of difficult place where Slumach might have spotted his gold: a narrow passageway would have required a small, thin person to be lowered down to pan for the gold, retrieve it and be pulled back up—all grist for a legend about a man who killed his helpers in order to keep his gold a secret.

Lovelace and Morrison, obviously excited, and Dan Gerak's father follow Dan to his seldom-seen creek, one that he says has little exposed bedrock and so much overgrowth it helps to "keep the place secret." He says this is the "one creek that shows gold," but that all the other gold seekers who come looking here for Slumach's gold miss it because the water is usually too high. At best, a prospector can get in and pan safely perhaps one or two days a year. Still, we are told (somewhat paradoxically) that if someone repeatedly panned around this area at the head of Pitt Lake, it would be just a matter of time before gold was found.

Lovelace's summary is succinct: "We found the secret valley. But the water is too high to find the motherlode." The documentary then wraps nicely with Gerak saying, "The creek is just calling out to find the gold." With that enticement, the grey-bearded Lovelace says he

Near the upper end of Pitt Lake, forbidding mountains rise sharply from the water's edge. One experienced searcher called this country "some of the worst topographical area in the province."

is ready for a return trip in which he'll explore deeper into the wilderness and make sure his timing is right for lower creek waters.

In a 2007 interview, Lovelace shared his perspective on searching for the hidden gold. "You have to be objective. A lot of people are fanatics about the lost mine. There's something about that area that can trick you." He reported that the DVD of the show on Slumach sold very well, and that their show garners a lot of attention from international adventurers, particularly Europeans. He expects to do a second feature on Slumach's lost mine that will reveal new facts and possibilities, and is continuing his research, based in part on the many queries and letters he received after the release of the first episode.

Lovelace plans to revisit the region soon, because there are more places to explore, one in particular. "We found an area that met all the criteria," Lovelace says of their first expedition. But it is not the only one that they feel has potential for gold. Dan's father, though he wasn't featured prominently in the television show, has explored the area extensively, and willingly shared his advice—and they've not yet followed up on all of it.

"When we next go exploring, we'll take all the right equipment. It's important to be able to film underwater. We have to do a specialized search, so that's what we'll do," he says with a pilot's confidence. "This second trip will have its own dangers, and there will be new perils with every weather change—and that's not to mention the curse."

At the end of his first episode on Slumach, a relaxed Lovelace is shown sitting alone on a riverbank. Looking out over the water, he asks no one in particular, "Is there gold in the Pitt River Valley?" He pauses for just a moment before answering his own question. "You bet there is—beyond your wildest dreams."

Rob Nicholson

Eleven searches later, the mine still proves elusive

Rob Nicholson's personal journey as a gold seeker began in 1987 when he was 20, and continues today. His *Lost Creek Mine* e-book (2003), his extensive website, his 11 searches for the mine's location and his willingness to share all he knows about the legend attest to his lifelong dedication to searching out the truth about Slumach and his legendary gold.

Nicholson's research began in earnest when he worked in a logging camp at Alvin, on the north Pitt River. Over two decades, he's made seven helicopter trips and four hiking expeditions into sites in Garibaldi and Golden Ears Provincial Parks. Along the way, he has struggled with the harsh territory and personal health challenges, but he adds much new material in his publication.

All the well-known names are there: Slumach, Jackson, Shotwell and Volcanic Brown, but two more are in the mix as well: Harrington and Stu Brown. Harrington comes to light in Nicholson's writings, and Stu Brown was introduced in both Nicholson's and Daryl Friesen's work.

Nicholson's account of the Jackson contribution to the legend notes that all records of bank deposits were destroyed in the San Francisco earthquake of April 18, 1906, making it virtually impossible to confirm either Jackson's existence or his deposit of gold in his bank account. Nicholson reports seeing, on one of his trips into the rough country at the head of Pitt Lake, a huge boulder that may be Jackson's tent-shaped rock, though it seems its dimensions would have warranted a mention in Jackson's letter. Nicholson's text reads:

> The particular "Jackson" rock to which I refer is in fact huge. It sits alone on a bench not far from Iceworm Creek and definitely seems to be out of place in its surroundings. It is similar in appearance and somewhat larger than the native "standing rock" west of Keremeos, B.C.

A lake at the foot of Stave Glacier. Volcanic Brown's last camp may have been found in this area.

The "Jackson" rock measures approximately 100 feet by 100 feet at the base by 70 feet in height. It has a slight overhang or lean in a southerly direction. On the ground a few feet out from the base but still just under the peak of the overhang are several very old fire pits spread out to form the shape of a semi-circle or arch.

At the base on one side of the "Jackson" rock is an obviously old depression measuring approximately 4 feet by 3 feet by 1 foot in depth. The depression is not a natural occurrence. The ground cover that has re-established itself over the depression suggests that the hole had been dug many decades earlier.

About 30 feet to one side of the "Jackson" rock are two slabs of rock leaning together that definitely give the appearance of a pup-tent. These slabs measure approximately 8 feet by 8 feet in length by 5 feet in height. One can actually crawl inside this natural rock structure.

What captures the attention of any Slumach aficionado is Nicholson's assertions about this being the rock whereof Jackson wrote:

I am fairly confident that this rock formation is the tent shaped rock that Jackson was referring to simply because of the hundreds of tent shaped rocks in the search area this is the only one that is definitely unique, can not be missed, and is within the travel distance identified in his letter. And these are the only two rocks on the entire bench.

No marks have been located or identified on either the "Jackson" rock or the tent shaped slabs. However, the inside of the slabs unfortunately were not examined. Jackson literally wrote that there was a mark cut out "in" the rock not "on" the rock. It has been suggested that the mark may actually be on the inside of the slabs. Only a re-examination of the site can determine if Jackson literally meant "in" or "on" the rock.

Nicholson then makes this startling revelation:

I have been independently advised that the ashes from the firepits were carbon dated a few years ago. The carbon dating results identified the ashes as being circa the very early 1800s.

Previous gold seekers have known Jackson was grubstaked by a Seattle man named Shotwell. Nicholson's research revealed that a man named Shotwell and a partner named Harrrington showed up in Ruskin, near Mission, in 1911, having returned from a long trek into the Pitt Lake country. The two men would have followed the Stave River from its headwaters down to the point where it joins the Fraser. They carried gold with them, according to reports from a Ruskin storekeeper.

In the matter of the curse, Nicholson courts controversy with a different interpretation. He suggests the translation of Slumach's legendary "Nika memloose, mine memloose" is "No man who finds the gold will live long enough to bring it out." This is much longer than

The Ruskin train station in 1910. Shotwell and Harrington reportedly boarded a train for Vancouver here after coming down the Stave River from the Stave Glacier area. And they reportedly carried gold with them!

the "When I die, mine dies" translation usually offered. We sought input on this discrepancy from First Nations people who know the languages involved. Their analysis: Chinook jargon contains similar words. "Nika-i" means "my" or "mine." "Memloose" means "to die" or "dead." The word "mine" was judged to be an English reference to the mine. Thus, "When I die, mine dies" appears to be correct.

Nicholson points to conflict (circa 1890) between Indians and prospectors in the Port Douglas area, leading to a new theory that Slumach may have been procuring women, thus accounting for some of the legendary disappearances. In Nicholson's words:

> Slumach may also have been independently trading or selling the native women to prospectors and trappers which again would not have been considered exceptional or abnormal for the time period. This scenario is not as likely to have occurred simply because Slumach did not speak English. He may however had some type of agreement with the Port Douglas natives in which they acted as trade brokers to the prospectors on his behalf.

In Nicholson's profile of R.A. Volcanic Brown, which culminates with his disappearance in 1931, he notes the "Volcanic" nickname came from his founding of the Volcanic claim north of Grand Forks, and his original find—which never paid off—is still known as Volcanic City. Nicholson says that Brown's other nickname, "Doc," came from his reputation as a natural healer, and from rumours that he plied a trade providing abortions. In his travels in the upper reaches of the mountains northeast of Pitt Lake, Nicholson came across a ruined cabin and, later, an old campsite that had an old stove, a mortar and pestle, and some food tins dating to the early part of the 1900s. These findings led Nicholson to believe that this site might well have been that of Volcanic Brown's last camp, where gold was found in a glass jar by his would-be rescuers.

Nicholson also speculates about Fire Mountain in the Lillooet area as another possible site for Volcanic Brown's last camp, noting that gold was discovered there in 1880. He writes:

This photo of Volcanic Brown appeared in the Vancouver *Province* on March 20, 1932, when the paper reported on the unsuccessful 27-day search for him in November 1931. It may have been taken in 1928 following his previous rescue, since his foot is bandaged. This damage likely slowed his progress into the mountains north of Pitt Lake in 1931.

Fire Mountain has been identified as being of significant interest to Game Warden Stevenson during the 1931 search for R.A. Brown. The history of Fire Mountain is not only interesting in the context of R.A. Brown, it is also significant to Jackson.

The initial discovery on Fire Mountain was during the early 1880s and Jackson's time period in question was between 1891 and 1906. It is distinctly probable, as previously mentioned, that Jackson was one of the countless prospectors drawn to the upper Harrison Lake country in search of their fortunes.

Nicholson then tells the story of Stu Brown (no relation to Volcanic), who wrote to the provincial government in 1974 claiming to have discovered rich gold deposits inside a provincial park (surmised to have been Garibaldi), with an estimated value ranging from $1 billion to $20 billion. Brown believed this was the legendary lost Pitt Lake mine, and had identified the site by reviewing aerial photos of the terrain in the Pitt Lake area. Brown felt that he discovered Jackson's find, but not Slumach's, nor that of Volcanic Brown. Nicholson says this about Stu Brown's find:

> The location itself is exactly like Jackson described it, except the canyon is shorter than a mile and one half. Seeing it from the same ridge that Jackson once stood on was an exhilarating experience. Brown describes a pool ... about twenty feet across and "ankle deep in gold" ... full of small nuggets.

Curiously, the text doesn't report Stu Brown proffering any samples as proof, but Rob Nicholson confirmed in our 2007 conversation that Brown had indeed brought out a five-pound nugget from the site. Trips back in to further prove the claim were thwarted by weather and illness challenges. Then Brown came up with a plan:

> Stu offered to hike into the site with me so that I could both see it for myself and independently document his discovery ... Stu's plan was for both of us to take two empty packsacks into

the site. We would fill one of the packsacks with nuggets, walk it out a short distance and leave it at a predetermined location. We would then walk back in and fill the second packsack, bringing it out to where the first one had been left. The object was to leap-frog the two packsacks out to the location of our vehicle.

Brown and Nicholson arrived very late in the day in the Fire Mountain area, and were about to embark on a two-day hike into the Terrarosa Glacier when they awoke to a heavy rain that had not been forecast. The downpour was so intense that the trip had to be cancelled. Nicholson writes: "Due to Stu's age and his progressively worsening Parkinson's disease, a planned trip the following year had to be cancelled." The reader will appreciate Nicholson's disappointment when he says, "I have not had the opportunity to return to the area."

Brown attempted to negotiate with both the government and a private mining corporation to bring out samples of gold from the site, with the stated honourable intention of using the find to reduce government debt. However, given the protected status of parks and the associated regulations against removing minerals from them, neither responded to his encouragement. In the end, ill health and the march of time precluded further trips.

In another chapter, Nicholson provides an interesting primer on basic geology, how gold is found, and which rock formations lead prospectors to expect a find:

> Gold is found in a wide variety of environments. Gold located in rock formations is commonly referred to as "vein gold." Vein gold is most commonly found in quartz veins, sulfide veins, and iron-stained rock that has been freed of sulfide. Displaced gold, commonly referred to as "placer gold," occurs when gold moves from its original host environment. Placer gold is most commonly found in creek and river beds. The prospector's rule of thumb for looking for the vein of placer gold is "the rougher the placer gold the closer the vein."

The Terrarosa Glacier, another of the high-country sites combed for gold. Was Slumach here?

Nicholson suggests that, given the different kinds of gold that the main protagonists in this story reported finding, there must have been multiple gold finds. He notes that reports of Slumach and Volcanic Brown having gold chipped out of a vein, Jackson finding "colours" (placer gold) and then nuggets, and Stu Brown also finding nuggets, all point to at least two and perhaps three different locations where gold has been found:

> The identification of two different types of gold circumstantially identifies two different locations of gold. In my opinion, there is a high probability that there are three separate gold deposits, independent of the other, that have been erroneously interconnected through the generality of the legend itself.

The lengthy timespans between the different finds also make it less likely that all were in the same place:

> Slumach brought a substantial quantity of gold into New Westminster on at least one occasion during the 1880s. Jackson wrote his infamous letter claiming ... to have found a creek, literally full of gold, sometime around the turn of the 19th century.

Shotwell and Harrington are on record as returning to civilization with an undetermined quantity of gold in 1911. Gold was found in R.A. "Doc" Brown's last known camp in 1931. In 1974, G.S. "Stu" Brown documents his claim to have found billions of dollars worth of gold in a location that matches the description given in Jackson's letter.

Nicholson reports that some spoilers, who have yet to find the mine themselves, have contaminated the area in order to dissuade competitors:

> These individuals readily admit to marking several large rocks with either the letter X or the letter J. These unscrupulous individuals also claimed to have flown over several areas and scattered hundreds of pounds of melted brass nuggets in countless different creeks. It was their assumption that if they could not find the legendary gold they would contaminate areas so badly that no one else would easily find it either.

The waters on either side of this quiet pool on a stream in Slumach country may churn and roil, and gold seekers must be cautious working their way through this area.

Nicholson's account wraps up with a collection of local myths, including one that says Slumach's ghost wanders the north Pitt Lake region, awaiting unwary searchers.

In our 2007 conversation, Nicholson said he has no doubt the mine exists in the area—in fact, he believes there are at least two locations: one with placer gold and the other vein gold. He suggests these locations are close to the "Jackson rock" and the pup-tent-shaped slabs in the Iceworm Creek area.

Finally, he believes it is unlikely Slumach had any connection to the mine or the legend that bears his name.

Glacier Lake, where Amanda Charnley reported Slumach had been given "a handful of bullets molded from gold."

A gold seeker views a glacier from a precarious perch.

A view of upper Pitt lake, where mountainsides rise steeply from the water.

Remnants of Research

In conducting research for our 1972 book and for this edition, we uncovered bits of information incidental to the Slumach story which, in the earlier book, comprised the chapter we called "Remnants of Research." With the continuing inflow of such information, this section has become one of the most interesting, because it contains many related elements of the lost mine stories that don't quite fit into the Slumach story, but do form part of the legend based on his life.

♦ ♦ ♦ ♦ ♦ ♦

Slumach has often been referred to as "John" or "Joe" Slumach. Aunt Mandy called him "Charlie." Throughout the court records of his trial and documents of his execution, he is referred to as "the Indian named Slumah," though newspaper accounts of the day consistently used Slumach.

♦ ♦ ♦ ♦ ♦ ♦

One of the most widely circulated photographs tied in with the story is one purported to be Slumach. It shows the face of a young man with a cap placed jauntily on his head. The best evidence available places Slumach's age at over 60—even as old as 80—when he came to public notice. The face in this photo appears to be of a man about 25 or 30 years old, which would place the date of the photograph (if it's Slumach, that is) somewhere in the 1830s or 1840s, when photography had not even been developed! This photograph was first published in *Liberty* in 1956, with C.V. Tench's article *The Gold Mine Murders of Nine British Columbia Women*. Where Tench dug up this obviously erroneous picture is anyone's guess.

◆◆◆◆◆◆

The three images of Slumach on page 125 have appeared in various publications and films. There are no authenticated images of him, but the photo of the older man with long grey hair on the left, a still from Michael Collier's docudrama *Curse of the Lost Gold Mine*, matches descriptions of him from early newspaper accounts of Louis Bee's murder. The photo of the young man wearing a cap is from a mid-1900s newspaper; it is highly unlikely that it is of Slumach. The sketch below it reflects an early description of him and is likely inaccurate as well.

◆◆◆◆◆◆

Slumach's executioner, described as a tall, thin character wearing a hood, is alleged to have been the same person who executed Louis Riel, the 19th-century Metis leader who led a rebellion against the Canadian government.

◆◆◆◆◆◆

Slumach's axe was of the type traded by the Hudson's Bay Company in the 1880s. A Dr. R.I. Bentley, who attended at his hanging, took it from Slumach's possessions. It was last known to belong to Dr. Bentley's great-grandson in Chilliwack.

◆◆◆◆◆◆

What did Slumach look like?

Slumach's axe, taken from his possessions after his hanging, is displayed with other items to show its relative size.

Whether anyone else besides Louis Bee died as a result of Slumach's alleged evil ways will always be a matter of conjecture. On September 10, 1898, a three-hour fire destroyed much of the residential and business districts of frontier New Westminster, turning to ash many records that might have shed light on the legend of Slumach's mine, including records belonging to Captain Pittendrigh.

◆ ◆ ◆ ◆ ◆ ◆

Logging companies have carried on operations in the past at various locations in the Pitt Lake area, and some still do. When we researched our 1972 edition, we found a report that Slumach once worked for one of those companies as a hunter. The report claimed that he would leave camp and return from an unknown location in an hour with fresh meat and a handful of gold nuggets.

One location mentioned is about halfway between Squamish and Pitt Lake. This story concerns an old prospector who lived for a time in Burnaby. His home was on a well-used trail, and travellers would frequently tell him of a gold mine to the northwest of Pitt Lake. The trail into the mine was fairly well marked for quite a distance, and then it suddenly disappeared. Those familiar with the trail knew that it picked up again just a few feet from this point, but its beginning was obscured by heavy brush. The second trail continued for a time until it too disappeared, only to pick up in a third trail nearby. This frustrating situation repeated itself all the way to the mine, and the few people who knew of the deliberate tricks in the trail found it easily, whereas others, of course, became befuddled and gave up.

Apparently this old prospector began to frequent the area. He once came across another prospector who had broken his leg and was near death because of a gangrenous infection. The dying prospector had with him a bag of gold nuggets, and told of the fabulously rich find he had made. He described it as being "up so high that nothing grows. As you stand by it you can see in the distant southeast Pitt Lake." He gave directions to the old prospector, and mentioned that the first person to find the gold had been an Indian man. The old prospector died without ever finding the mine.

Other hints to the mine's location—presumably valuable only to an Aboriginal person, given that the curse supposedly says no White person will ever find the mine and live—have come to light. Here are three hints we discovered in our 1972 research (see illustrations by Fred Bosman on page 128). The first was something reportedly seen by a group of prospectors camping near Gold Creek, which flows into the west side of Alouette Lake. It only occurred once, in the rays of the setting sun. Although they were very familiar with the mountainous area, they had never seen the sight before, nor have they seen it since:

- The gold lies under a mountain that appears to be the shape of a sleeping maiden, hands on her breasts.
- When you paddle north past Large Goose Island on Pitt Lake, look 45 degrees to the southeast—towards Haney. On top of the mountains you can see the Indian head (from forehead to Adam's apple). Beneath this mountain is the gold.
- When you hike toward Bridal Veil Falls, look straight across the lake and see the faces of a sleeping Indian and his woman. They appear to be lying down. When you stand so that their noses line up, you are standing on a line along which the mine can be found.

◆ ◆ ◆ ◆ ◆ ◆

The *Daily Columbian* report of Slumach's trial on November 14, 1890, mentions that defence counsel asked for Slumach's case to be adjourned on the grounds that two important witnesses for the defence, "Florence Reid and Moody" could not be "obtained" in time for the trial. It has been suggested that this Moody may have been an illegitimate offspring of Colonel Richard Clement Moody, but Colonel Moody left British Columbia in 1863, and a George Moody, thought to be the witness in question, was born in 1875, the son of a Native woman and Sewell Prescott Moody, the first large-scale

These three sketches were based on descriptions of landmarks pointing to the location of Slumach's mine.

lumber exporter in B.C. Although both witnesses were present at Slumach's trial, the defence counsel did not call them.

◆◆◆◆◆◆

Over the years, the Slumach legend has provided fodder for screenplays, short stories and novels, most of which were never published—with one exception. In 2006, more than 20 years after author Edgar Ramsey began to write it, *Slumach: The Lost Mine* weaves together two threads: an anthropology professor's interest in writing a book on the legend, and two miscreants' plan to get rich quick with a trek into the Pitt Lake wilderness to find the gold. Some sex, gore and mysterious happenings from an unknown source are thrown into the mix, and when the two teams converge at the head of the lake, this pulp-fiction telling sheds a different light on the Slumach legend.

◆◆◆◆◆◆

Exhibit Eh! is a fun television escapade shown on the CTV Travel Channel and hosted by Todd Macfie and Frank Wolf, who roam the country "exposing Canada, one mystery at a time." Slumach's story was an inevitable lure, and their 23-minute episode, created in 2007, begins with them hunkering down in the New Westminster Public Library, apparently engaged in diligent research—all aimed at finding a "stash of gold" that no one has been able to find.

They report that "40 people have succumbed to the curse," and hedge their own bets by going to Pitt Lake country under the guidance of two known prospectors, who take them to the "golden mountains" and caution that "gold is usually in the worst spot." Bravely, they don headlamps and enter a long, deep mine shaft. They chisel away as instructed, but leave empty-handed.

Finally, the hosts caution other would-be prospectors with sage, if peculiar, advice about the rugged topography: "What is not straight up, is usually straight down."

◆◆◆◆◆◆

Newspaper articles from the 1940s reported on searches for the mine in that decade. A 1940 item from the *Maple Ridge—Pitt Meadows Gazette* covers a search being launched by Mrs. Al Jenkins of Pitt Lake, who headed up the lake looking for Slumach's mine. There is no follow-up article to tell of her success or failure. The same newspaper featured a 1941 article reporting that Gordon Dalrymple of Websters Corners had found the mine three months earlier (than the publication of the article). Dalrymple claimed other searchers were "all in the wrong place," but gives no further information on his supposed find. This article provides some recollections, recounted some three decades after the fact, from Hugh Murray, who had guided some seekers into the area to the northeast of the head of Pitt Lake around 1912. It mixes up two names, Johnson and Jackson, while relating Jackson's adventure. Another article, this one from 1945, recounts the rescue of Joe Eaves, a prospector from Silver Creek who became ill while searching in the Widgeon Lake area and was rescued by an RCAF plane. The item also tells of a San Francisco man named John Bruno who brought out some $9,000 in gold in 1907. This was in the same decade in which Jackson reportedly found his gold. The evident confusion in this mid-20th-century reporting doubtless contributed to the plethora of mixed messages about the search for the mine.

♦ ♦ ♦ ♦ ♦ ♦

If you google "Slumach," you'll find that more than 2,200 results come up in less than half a second—all of those for a local legend about a lost gold mine centred around Pitt Lake in British Columbia, Canada! When we began researching the legend in 1972, there was no web, no Google, no search engines, only the local newspaper archives and the legislative library in Victoria. More than three decades later, the web is alive with tales, listserves, web versions, maps, histories and opinions, some perhaps accurate, many more inaccurate.

♦ ♦ ♦ ♦ ♦ ♦

Professional film and video makers have engaged in these Slumach-treks for years; today amateur video makers chronicle their expeditions into the wilds of the Pitt Lake country searching for the mine, and then post their productions on the Internet. We can expect to see more of the same in this age of blogs, personal websites and shared information.

♦♦♦♦♦♦

On the shores of the upper Pitt River at Alvin, site of a hatchery and near where Corbold Creek enters the river, there's a rather comfortable place to stay. Pitt River Lodge is not for those who hesitate to spend a few extra dollars to make sure they have solid walls about them and a sturdy roof over their heads. Gold seekers never had it so good!

The lodge's website, www.pittriverlodge.com/index.htm, features a fine rendition of the Slumach story on the page "Lost Gold Mine," and an engaging history of the area's settlement, on and off, over the past century. Doubtless, evenings around the lodge's fireplace are filled with stories of Slumach's legendary lost hoard, which is supposedly hidden within the surrounding peaks.

♦♦♦♦♦♦

International interest in the Slumach story ran high in 2005, when the German film *Auf Slumachs Spuren* (*On Slumach's Trails*) recounted a search for the mine. One source reported that this film received exceptionally high ratings on German television.

♦♦♦♦♦♦

Fred Braches was at Don Waite's place on a drizzly Saturday morning in February 2007, when author Rick Antonson dropped by for a visit.

"I heard you'd be here, so I came," began Fred. "First, I read your book from 1972. I saw you treated Slumach with respect. I'm looking for Slumach. Not looking for gold. Nice to meet you." He handed Rick a coffee, and the three sat and began an easy conversation.

Notes from the interview with Waite that morning are interspersed with observations by Fred. When we talked about Slumach's hanging, Fred sat forward on the couch and gave his opinion that the half-day trial was "exceedingly short." He opened a leather case that held two photocopies of a document.

"I brought you each one of these. It's a copy of the judge's procedure notes and the hanging certificate. I finally tracked them down in the Ottawa archives."

Spidery handwriting filled the white spaces around the printed document's framed words:

Department of the Secretary of State, Canada.

Address: *New Westminster B.C.*

Name: *Hon. Mr. Justice Drake*

Date: *15/24 Nov. 1890*

Heading: *Capital Case of Sumah (or Shumah)*

Among the pages was a copy of a Canadian Pacific Railway Company's telegram that read: "Your letter ... in reference to the execution of the Indian Sumach received this day ... " We flipped through Fred's gift while he added to his observations.

"You know, there's no record of Bee's death certificate. And Bee's wife, Kitty, is the only one to speak about him at the trial." Fred shifted his glasses and settled back on the couch.

"Slumach should have pleaded self-defence," he continued.

We all nodded in agreement.

"And the sketch in your book from 1972 shows four people in the canoe when Slumach shot Bee. Change that. There were only two—Bee and an Indian from Harrison River named Seymour."

Fred sat quietly as Waite reminisced at length about his trips to Pitt Lake. When Waite was done, Fred said he thought that Slumach should have been spared capital punishment because of his old age.

To back up his assertions that the Slumach story has been wildly distorted, Fred is compiling copies of as much original 1890s material related to Slumach's trial as he can put his hands on. He wants to concentrate on the people and the time, rather than the legends. It is his intention to ferret out every document tucked within archives or found, copied or kept by scholars or fellow researchers. "The Slumach story has grown to a collection of legends of epic proportions, and it is time that we go back to the source and the simple facts," he said.

Braches has posted a set of primary sources online regarding Slumach, the man, and his trial, adding some commentary to those records and the sad events they tell about. "On my website [www.slumach.ca], I'm sharing the records I've found and will add to the collection as new material comes to me. That information is there for all to use and appreciate. There's no commerce in binding this information for resale, although I am planning to make a desktop version available."

Fred wouldn't let us go without talking about the speculation that Slumach had gold, of a sort.

"The Harrison Indians are rumoured to have told Slumach where the mine was," he began. "That accounts for stories he had half a sugar bag filled with nuggets. Slumach had let them use his canoe. So if he did have gold, he'd likely have gotten it second-hand from them. In that case, it wasn't even Pitt Lake gold. It was Harrison Lake gold."

Not that he believes Slumach had anything to do with gold:

"You already suggested in your book from 1972 that the newspaper people at the time of the crime would have had a field day if there was any reason to connect Slumach with gold findings—there is nothing of that kind mentioned in the 1890s records."

As the coffee and the morning both ran out, Fred prepared to leave. He did so with an admonition: "You're writers. Often, not all the facts go through as truth. Readers deserve to know the difference between healthy skepticism and fabricated stories. That motivates me to seek what was behind the man behind the legend."

◆◆◆◆◆◆

This was not the last we would hear from Fred Braches. As our research work continued, he provided us his views on a variety of topics. He revisited the August 1926 edition of the Sunday *Province*, which published an interview with Jason Allard about Slumach, and wrote to us as follows:

Jason Allard, "who knows everything there is to be known about Fraser Valley Indians," according to the *Province*, knew Slumach "the desperado" by repute, and he claimed to have been one of Slumach's jailers. Allard believed that Slumach and his brother were born in Nanaimo, although their father came from the Pitt Lake and Pitt River area. Living up the Nanaimo River, Slumach murdered any stragglers coming his way for the

Jason Ovid Allard, interpreter at the Slumach trial, and possibly Slumach's jailer.

only reason that he "liked to be monarch of all he surveyed." Caught in the act of killing "an Indian," he escaped by playing dead in his canoe and with his brother moved to Pitt Lake and there, living like hermits, murdered "everyone that ventured into their territory … One can picture the wild terror of being hunted by this long-haired strange creature." That went on until Slumach was caught and sentenced to die for killing Louis Bee.

Allard told the interviewer that "when Slumach was first captured, he behaved just as any wild creature would do." Allard remembered that the long-haired Slumach "had wonderfully large eyes which reminded of the eyes of a grey lynx." Later in the article, we read that Slumach "was not given to talk and never boasted about the number of scalps he had taken." In the eyes of many in those days, Slumach was a savage. On the other hand, Allard described Slumach as a "most charming personality, with the manners of a French dancing master … [who] continued to exhibit the same good manners" during his time in jail.

Slumach's name, according to Allard, was actually Slough Mough, which means rain, and he also suggested that Slumach's brother's name was S'mamqua or "ceremonial undertaker," a name Allard thought very appropriate because this brother "always chose the graveyard to do his courting." The surname Bee of the victim, "half-breed Kanaka" Louis Bee, is interpreted by Allard as Poll-al-ee.

About the "secret of a great gold mine" the reporter adds: "Had Mr. Allard only known that his prisoner knew of its existence, he might have become a very wealthy man, for the murderer, with his fine manners, would undoubtedly have told him where it was."

Braches wrote that although it was broadcaster/critic Clyde Gilmour who introduced the murders of women into the Slumach story in 1947, it was a different author who gave the women names.

Molly Tynan and her ilk were the brain children of the prolific fiction writer C.V. Tench, who published in such periodicals as *Boys Own Paper, Daredevil Detective Stories, Western Action, Ranch Romance* and *True West*, to mention just a few.

His version of the Slumach story, *The Gold Mine Murders of Nine British Columbia Women*, appeared in the *Annals of Canadian Crime* section of the Canadian edition of *Liberty* in July 1956. The article is illustrated with photographs supposedly of some of the victims, as well as one of a fictitious British Columbia constable, Eric Grainger, who, posing as a gold prospector, solved the case. It also includes a photo presented as that of the "slayer of the nine women," "John" Slumach, who was hanged for his crimes in New Westminster's provincial jail. "Raw gold by the handful" says one caption, and "All his girlfriends drowned," says another.

The names of some of the girls are Tillie Malcom, Susan Jesner, Mary Warne and that of his last victim, Molly Tynan, whose body was brought up in a net, conveniently bearing a hunting knife still "embedded in her heart." The knife was identified by Slumach's fingerprints found on the handle [according to the article.] However, it is unlikely that the New Westminster police would have used fingerprinting for identification in the same year the technology was introduced by Scotland Yard, therefore, in recounts of the story, Slumach is indentified as the murderer when his mother recognized the knife as his.

Braches went on reflect on the person at the centre of the legend:

Who was the real Slumach? Was he indeed the "bloodthirsty old villain" of the newspaper reports? In her interviews, Aunt Mandy stressed that her parents (Peter and Katherine Pierre) said that Slumach was a kind old man, closer to 80 than to 60, and that he was a crippled and harmless old widower who lived in a shack at the bottom end of Pitt Lake, on the abandoned Silver Creek Indian Reserve.

Why, then, did this kind, elderly man shoot Bee? Louis Bee was described as "in the habit of blustering at and threatening everyone with whom he came in contact." Slumach reportedly also told Jason Allard "that the young man who he killed had tantalized him on every occasion." It was said that there was "bad blood between Slumach and Bee." Bee's words that day may have been the last straw, enough to enrage Slumach to the point that he shot and killed him with his old front loader.

Was Slumach a serial killer? There were rumours in the press at the time of his conviction that this was not the first time Slumach had killed, but as Aunt Mandy said: "It all started with all the lies they said about him. He was this and that, you know, a cruel old man and all that." Indian Agent McTiernan believed Slumach, who denied that he had killed anyone other than Louis Bee. The buzz may have related to a number of reportedly unsolved murders in the area for which Slumach's hanging was meant to be a deterrent, aside from punishment for his own crime.

With the hanging of this old man, the press's interest in Slumach died. What else was there to report? Slumach was only *rumoured* to be involved with other murders, and at that time there was nothing about gold in his story. British Columbia, between the Fraser and Klondike gold rushes, was a world full of prospectors, fortune seekers and speculators, and even gossip about gold would have triggered a stampede to the Pitt Lake area. That would have been duly recorded by the press—but it was not—it did not happen.

There is some debate over whether Slumach shot Bee in self-defence, because Bee was wielding an axe when he approached him, (Don Waite had noted that Aunt Mandy Charnley told him, "Bee came at Slumach with an axe.") Waite is inclined to "believe her version over that of Seymour's, being fully aware of what the police, etc., could have told Seymour to say at the trial." Fred Braches counters that while Aunt Mandy's remarks about an axe-wielding Bee do not match testimony at the trial, nor do they match descriptions of Bee's shot wound. He suggests an axe-wielding Bee would have suffered a frontal shot, and not one "at the shoulder, going down through the heart and lung," which was described by Dr.

This rifle is similar to the one Slumach used to murder Louis Bee in 1890.

Walker, who performed the autopsy on Bee's body. Braches concludes that Dr. Walker's testimony "is consistent with Charlie Seymour's witness account of the murder."

◆ ◆ ◆ ◆ ◆ ◆

In our 1972 edition of *Slumach's Gold*, we introduced the coverage in the *Daily Columbian* of the Louis Bee murder by noting, "The most reliable information on Slumach is found in the press records of 1890–91." Fred Braches has since suggested that calling the *Daily Columbian's* information "reliable" is too strong an endorsement. He explains:

The reliability of the press as a source of information is immediately put in question by the account of the murder in the *Daily Columbian*'s first report in September 1890, a version repeated in January 1891 after the hanging of Slumach. What is reported in the press is quite different from what is recorded at the inquisitions and the trial. If, as reported in the newspaper story, there were "several other Indians" around when Bee was murdered, they all would have been called to witness. In truth there was only one witness to the murder, a man called Seymour, from Harrison, and it is on his pronouncement that Slumach was convicted. This Seymour lived in a fishing camp at Lillooet (now Alouette) Slough together with Louis Bee, their wives and an unnamed old man. On that fateful day, Bee and Seymour set out to find bait for their sturgeon line. They heard a shot and went to see who was shooting and what the shooter was hunting. Sitting in their canoe alongside the shore they encountered Slumach, who was standing on the bank with a single-barrelled muzzle loader in his hand. Some words were spoken, Slumach fired, and Bee's dead body dropped overboard into the river. Slumach went to his own canoe and started reloading his gun. Seymour fled over land, recovered his canoe later and reported the murder to the Indian Agent Peter McTiernan at New Westminster that same night.

◆ ◆ ◆ ◆ ◆ ◆

The earliest printed mention of the Slumach legend that we found while researching our 1972 publication was in the April 3, 1906, edition of the *Daily Province*. Fred Braches resurrected it as we were editing this book. Under the headline "Buried Treasure at Pitt Lake," the story says "that it would appear that some man by the name of Frazier secured information that an old man, who has ere this been gathered to his rest [a lovely expression from turn-of-that-century language], had some valuable placer grounds in the Pitt Lake country. He had recovered $8,000 in gold nuggets and these he had hidden under a rock. He had then passed away, but had left directions where the treasure and the placer ground had to be found."

That news came to the knowledge of others who set out to find the gold "ahead of another party which was stampeding to the treasure ground." Of course nothing was found. They all had a hard time though: "The party had a very rough trip as the weather was rainy, and sleeping out did not remind one of the dreams between Dutch feathers."

Might the man who recovered "$8,000 in gold nuggets" and left it "hidden under a rock" be Jackson? This would be but two years after his reported trek into the rugged country northeast of Pitt Lake, and the verbal clues match those in his famous letter.

Legend has it that a Constable Eric Grainger tried to thwart Slumach's attentions to Molly Tynan, but there is no mention of this in court records or anywhere else. Grainger may be the completely fictitious construct of an over-enthusiastic author.

This pictograph is near Pitt Lake. One source claims it profiles the legend of "Slumack" or "Shumack."

Epilogue

"They found Slumach's lost mine," Rikk Taylor had told us over lunch that autumn day as we sat in The Keg restaurant awed by a zip-lock bag of quartz, sparkling dust and the validating assay report. He grinned. "See for yourselves," he said, as much a dare as a direction.

"Where?" one of us asked.

"When?" blurted the other.

"I'll get to that," he said, "because it's not where you think it is. It's not where people have been looking."

Rick tested the heft of the rock in his hand. "This could be from Stave Glacier. That's where Volcanic Brown spent his last trip, and he found gold."

Rikk smirked. "Brown was wrong. Miles wrong. He was mountains away from where Slumach found gold."

"Brown *had gold*," Brian said.

"Some nuggets," clarified Rikk. "He just had some nuggets."

True. Brown could have had gold along with him from elsewhere.

"Brown was high up on the Stave Glacier," said Rikk, who then pointed at our gold, "Certainly not where this came from."

We smiled at one another, and then asked Rikk, "Where'd you find this?"

"First off, I didn't find it. Oh, I did chisel out these rocks, and kept some for myself. But I accomplished that climbing around a finished mine site. They didn't leave much. It was cleaned out pretty good. Gold makes people thorough," he said. "Crazy, but thorough."

The server placed our salads down. Drinks arrived, and we clinked glasses in a toast: "To Slumach."

"Who are 'they' who found the mine?"

Rikk hesitated a few moments. "I got a phone call."

Oh, how many of our own tips or stories had begun that same way. "Late at night?" Brian laughed.

"Yes. Late at night," said Rikk.

We put down our utensils and waved the server away.

Rikk began his story. "A fellow I know dabbled in mining all his life. We've grown old together swapping Slumach tales and guesses. He never gave up looking. Never stopped believing. He got a lead from two miners who'd found a vein—a profitable vein. That was several years ago. Then they went quiet on us."

The restaurant was noisy, so Rikk leaned across the table as we hunched over to hear his whisper.

"Harrison Lake," he said.

"Harrison?"

He nodded repeatedly as our hushed voices checked off the list of likelier sites. "Not Corbold Creek? Not Stave Glacier? Not Pitt Lake?"

"Harrison Lake," he affirmed, picking up his fork.

When his miner friend next heard from the two prospectors, they told him they'd cleared their find of gold-bearing rock. They had crushed and carted away what they wanted and then processed it into flat bars of gold. They'd left the area as one might expect: untidy and untended, since it no longer held value for them. So they told Rikk's old miner friend where it was. The two of them ventured out one weekend in a four-by-four to the east side of Harrison Lake, to a point on a logging road where, clued by a landmark, they tried to get off the road and into the mine site. After three aborted attempts, their scratched vehicle forced through brush, veered around a large tree and onto a barely passable trail that showed old tire ruts.

"It was there all right," Rikk continued. "Dug, carved ... indications of some blasting, a foot of heavy tire tracks from a grinder left rusting under a tree—everything else was washed by rains, smoothed by two winters' snow."

We sat there in awe: gold in a plastic satchel, a dated assay report and a man known for his integrity—all at the same table.

"We chipped away all weekend, certain we were in Slumach's footsteps," Rikk said. "Jackson never found this, nor did Tiny Allen. Volcanic Brown may have trekked near there on his way to the Pitt, but if he'd found traces, he'd have pitched his tent, prospected a while and lived a wealthy life."

That prompted the next question: "How much?"

"Millions," he replied. "The gold mine was worth millions."

Suddenly, from all those decades before, we could hear the warning as the old fisherman's wife leaned her frail body over a campfire: "There's a lost gold mine ... but you'll never find it—'least not find it and live."

Rikk's voice broke the silence. "You should go there." He was visibly tiring from his post-stroke weakness and the animated conversation. "Camp overnight at the mine," he said. "If nothing else, you'll feel the presence of Slumach's ghost. We did."

Our lunch was over and Rikk prepared to leave. We would never see him again.

Before he left, he did something both Slumach and Jackson would have admired. He picked up a napkin and set it between us. When he removed a pen from his pocket, we knew a special moment was about to unfold. Then he said, "Let me draw you a map ... "

Gold nuggets, the stuff of dreams for gold seekers everywhere.

On How Firm a Ground?

The case of Slumach and his gold is not closed, nor is it likely it ever will be. Any legend has its roots in some kind of truth—but just where the truth lies in this particular legend will still be a cause for conjecture years from now.

Surely Jackson, Shotwell and Slumach each have their places in this fascinating tale, but are they places given them by historical fact, or were they merely characters who unwittingly slipped into what is no more than a local legend?

We hear of dozens of men who have died in the attempt to find Slumach's lost mine; have they died chasing a wild dream fabricated by a fertile imagination or two, or have they died with the secret cache only yards or perhaps feet from their fingertips?

Readers must decide for themselves on how firm a ground the various theories concerning the mine stand, and in that same vein, we feel we ought to share *our* individual feelings about the truth behind the legend. In 1972, at the risk of eating our words at some future date, we summed up our views. We present them here again, and have added our updated perspectives.

No doubt new information will come to light that will support or supplant the material found in this book. Until then, we trust our book fulfills its intended purpose to present an interesting, informative, and realistic look at one of the most intriguing legends over three centuries—certainly an outstanding chapter in British Columbia's history.

In 1972 Rick Antonson wrote:

So here we are at the end of over two years of research, with no conclusive evidence that proves Slumach did have a mine or didn't have a mine. It is more than obvious that the facts behind the story have been distorted to, in some cases, gross exaggerations. Two points, however, are clear: the first is that Slumach *did* live, and that he was hung for Louis Bee's murder. The second point is that no records can be found anywhere to prove that he at any time had any gold in large proportions.

Have 23 people been fools, or maybe 28, or 36? Did they not pay heed to the lack of extensive evidence about Slumach's mine? The only proof to the mystery is the mine itself, and we may never know for sure if it exists or not.

In 2007 Rick Antonson wrote:

Now, 35 years later, after fresh starts and false starts by a host of diligent gold seekers who have shared their findings, I arrive at a more solid conclusion.

Unless you believe Aunt Mandy's story that Slumach scrawled a rough map on his death cell's concrete bench and showed it to Peter Pierre, no person's words link Slumach to gold. If the story was true and Pierre believed Slumach, it is certainly likely that Pierre could have slipped, fallen and broken his hip, as Aunt Mandy said, while in Pitt country, maybe or maybe not looking for gold. Regardless, it is a short leap of faith for me to imagine his laughter at the circumstances of his mishap. One can almost hear his words: "Ol' Slumach must've placed a curse on this area."

That scenario, with its thin thread to facts, ties Slumach to the curse and to the gold. I want to believe in that linkage because it is fun and tenable and is the root of a legend. It sits well beside the available evidence that suggests Slumach never had gold in sufficient quantity to arouse suspicion, let alone in sufficient amounts to prompt press coverage. Yet it also squares with the possibility that he found slivers of gold to pry out of a rock with his knife—once or twice.

I believe Rikk Taylor's words "They found gold—and there was lots." He had reconciled a legitimate gold find in the Harrison Lake area with gold from a century-old legend that he loved as much as we do. And he said what he wanted to believe was true: "They found Slumach's lost mine." Frankly, I don't hold that statement to be correct—I don't believe it was Slumach's gold they found.

Unless ...

In 1972 Brian Antonson wrote:
The hero of this work, Slumach, certainly did live, and certainly did die a murderer's death—this much is a matter of public record. But after two years of research and investigation, we are still unable to show any evidence that points to Slumach being the owner of a secret gold mine. There is so much overwhelming evidence *against* Slumach's ownership, that it would seem the legend of Slumach's Lost Creek gold mine is just that—a legend.

However, there is enough evidence to show that there may be a treasure trove in those unforgiving mountains yet. If Jackson's story can be held as true, or if Volcanic Brown's last camp makes any more than simple mute testimony to the existence of gold somewhere in that region, or if Tiny Allen's excited glimpse into the mother-creek of the lode is to be accepted, then there must be gold in "them thar hills."

I believe that Slumach is the unwitting hero of an intriguing legend—not through his choice, but through the mishap of history. Legends find their roots in many different places, and by some accidental connection that we of this day may never know about, Slumach was once thrown into the midst of a legendary bullring.

If there is any gold, it is to be found in the high reaches near the headwaters of Corbold Creek—perhaps as far up as Stave Glacier, near the site of Volcanic Brown's last camp, but I don't believe that Slumach knew of any gold in that region, nor did he murder because of it.

Unwitting hero he,
Who murdered Louis Bee,
But all the rest,
Is just pure jest,
A joke on you and me.

In 2007 Brian Antonson wrote:
That's the way I wrapped it up 35 years ago. This time, it's different. We are not alone. Other gold seekers are out there, and they're writers. Bill Barlee, Rob Nicholson, Daryl Friesen, Jack Mould, Don Waite, Garnet Basque, Tom Paterson—their tomes have stocked the shelves of bookstores across the land, and grace web pages and CDs in a more contemporary age.

Yes, I believe there is gold to be found in the high country at the head of Pitt Lake, but, sadly, there's no way to prove that. Follow any thread and it comes to a dead end. Jackson found gold, but finding Jackson has been a challenge, though his letter still circulates and perhaps so do his maps. Volcanic Brown found gold—it was there in his last camp—but did he bring that with him from another find or did it originate in the high country near Stave Glacier? Rikk Taylor's report showed gold, but it came from near Harrison Lake, not Pitt. Jack Mould found a mine, perhaps worked by Spaniards centuries ago, but its location is many miles away from the traditional search area near Bute Inlet. Stu Brown found gold once near Fire Mountain, but couldn't reach it again. Donna thought she discovered Jackson's find, but also discovered that it had been played out by someone else—with a backhoe, no less! I've seen photographs of different tent-shaped rocks shot by different people in different locations, all purporting to be *the one*. Tiny Allen and Alfred Gaspard may just be two names among many who might have stumbled on a strike in the forbidding country around Pitt Lake.

And so it goes, tale after tale after tale, each just maddeningly out of reach, each just one step removed from confirmation and attribution, all in the frustrating domain of the unknown and unknowable.

I want to believe gold exists in the upper Pitt. I want place names like Alvin and Corbold and Stave to haunt the minds of treasure seekers for years to come. I want to believe that those lives lost in searching for the gold have not been lost in vain, that there's more to the whole story than some old legends cobbled together around the unknown grave of a hanged murderer. I want to believe someone yet will stumble upon a creek, ankle-deep in gold nuggets, flowing rich, waiting to be relieved of its fortune.

And I want this story to continue to unfold. I want new gold seekers to study the evidence and continue the search. I want people to read this and other books about the topic, to keep the fire of inquiry burning. I want new minds to sift through new evidence and ask new questions, to dig deep, and then deeper still. And I want there to be reason one day for a follow-up book titled *We Found Slumach's Gold!*

In 1972 Mary Trainer wrote:
After carefully scrutinizing our compilation of facts and theories, some readers will no doubt find themselves thinking the entire legend is a hoax. No wonder.

With no connection between Slumach and his gold mentioned until 10 years after his hanging, it does seem highly probable that either there never was any gold, or that Slumach confided his secret to one or two close friends, and the facts are now exaggerated far out of proportion. After all, he may have accidentally found only a few nuggets and fabricated a gigantic yarn entirely for his own amusement, or—more fun yet—he may have constructed the whole tale to buffalo some gullible, greedy White men into running wildly into the bush seeking a non-existent treasure.

Geologists say it is doubtful that gold could be found in the Pitt Lake area, but during the Barkerville boom 40 years earlier, a miner could have cached his hoard away and never returned for it, only to have Slumach stumble upon it years later.

Anyway, the next time you're bored, and feel the urge for a little adventure ...

In 2007 Mary Trainer wrote:

What's wonderful about Slumach's legend is its enduring romance, which continues to appeal 35 years later.

I still remember the twinkle in the eyes of "Century Sam," a caricature of a grizzled early-gold-rush prospector who was the mascot of British Columbia's centennial in 1958.

That infectious twinkle endures in the eyes of 21st-century gold seekers. It's the tease that draws them—the possibilities of the find. It's the 19th-century version of online gambling or the popular TV show *Deal or No Deal*. After all, how much thrill can be experienced hunkered down in front of a computer or TV, when a complete body-mind adventure beckons from the ruggedness above Pitt Lake?

I love pondering the intriguing "greed" factor surrounding the Slumach legend. Many gold seekers in this book claim they know the mine's location. But think about it. If you were one of those intrepid folks, why would you *ever* tell anyone, make a map or share any knowledge whatsoever that would enable "the other guy" to benefit? It just makes sense that you would want to keep your information to yourself. What better way to obscure the trail than by falsifying your findings and publishing them?

We'll never know if any one gold seeker has actually found the lode and has quietly packed out their prize without saying a word—a much more likely scenario, in my view.

Still, I'm betting that the elusive, unsolved mystery of the mine will continue to inveigle dreamers everywhere. It adds a magical charm to B.C.'s history. Century Sam would love it.

Appendix A: A Slumach Timeline

1890—Slumach murders Louis Bee and first appears in the local press.

1891—Slumach is hanged for Bee's murder.
Based on what Amanda Charnley told Don Waite, Peter Pierre is believed to have searched for some gold possibly belonging to his uncle, Slumach. The first mention of a curse may have originated at this time.

1901—W. Jackson finds gold northeast of the head of Pitt Lake and sends a description of the location to the Seattle man who grubstaked him, a Mr. Shotwell.

1904—W. Jackson dies in San Francisco, after having deposited thousands of dollars in gold in his bank.

1906—The first article on the legend of Slumach's gold appears in the *Daily Province* on April 3. The find is attributed to an "old man" who sounds very much like Jackson.

1911—Shotwell and Harrington reportedly arrive at Ruskin train station with gold, having come down the Stave River, perhaps from the Stave Glacier. Both reportedly die shortly after returning to Seattle.

1925—The Sunday *Province* of August 9 carries an article on "The Lost Mine of Pitt Lake," citing Shotwell as the character now believed to have been Jackson.

1928—Volcanic Brown fails to return from searching for the mine and is rescued by a volunteer search team.

1931—Volcanic Brown again fails to return from searching for the mine. A volunteer search team finds only his last camp, with 11 ounces of raw gold. Brown is never seen again.

1940s—Various newspaper articles appear about searches for the mine.

1950s—Alfred Gaspard disappears while searching for the mine.
—Various newspaper articles about searches for the mine continue to appear.

1958—An American network television program, *Treasure*, brings the Slumach legend into the spotlight, showing a search for the mine near Spindle Canyon.

1960—Lewis Hagbo's death is reported in the press. The article suggests he may have been the 23rd person to die while searching for the mine.

1961—*The Columbian* launches a weekend search near Sheridan Hill in Pitt Meadows.

1960s—Tiny Allen finds a tent-shaped rock, then dies before returning to the site where he found it.

—Various newspaper articles about searches for the mine continue to appear.

1970—Bill Barlee tells the Slumach story in *Canada West* magazine.

1972—The first book about the legend, *In Search of a Legend: Slumach's Gold*, is published.

 Don Waite tells the Slumach story in his book *Kwant'stan*.

1976—"Legend of the Lost Creek Mine" by T.W. Paterson appears in *Canadian Treasure Trails*.

1981—Heritage House publishes *Slumach's Gold: In Search of a Legend*, a compilation of several earlier works.

1983—The *Province* and CKVU report on a week-long search for the mine in the Widgeon Creek area at the southwest corner of Pitt Lake.

1985—Gold seeker Norm searches in country northeast of the head of Pitt Lake and shows author Brian Antonson photos of a tent-shaped rock around which he found gold.

1990s—A German television series *Treasure Hunters* tells the Slumach story and searches for the mine northeast of Pitt Lake.

1992—Elizabeth Hawkins' story of Jack Mould's lifelong search for Slumach's gold mine is published.

1995—Gold seeker Donna and her husband search for the mine. An account in the *Vancouver Sun* says they found it, but it had already been worked out.

1996—Michael Collier's docudrama, *Curse of the Lost Gold Mine*, airs on Canadian network television.

2000 (circa)—Former publisher of *The Columbian*, Rikk Taylor, informs Brian and Rick Antonson that the mine has been found and worked out, near the east shore of Harrison Lake.

2001—Gold seeker Daryl Friesen launches his e-book about his lifelong search for the mine.

2003—Gold seeker Rob Nicholson launches his e-book about his lifelong search for the mine.

2005—The German film *Auf Slumachs Spuren* (*On Slumach's Trails*) recounts a search for the mine.

—John Lovelace produces a *Wings Over Canada* episode on the Slumach legend and the search for the mine.

Appendix B: The History of Pitt Lake

Pitt Meadows is part of the Katzie First Nation's traditional territory. White people began to explore the area between 1837 and 1858, and it was officially organized on September 12, 1847. It was incorporated on April 23, 1914.

The city of Pitt Meadows is situated to the west of Maple Ridge, and is bounded by Pitt River on the west, Pitt Polder on the north, the Katzie Reserve and Fraser River on the south, and Katzie Slough on the east. Elevation varies between 25 feet and 300 feet above sea level.

In the area's early development, young Dutch farming couples immigrated to Canada and purchased rundown dairies from the Mennonites, who were occupying the area at the time. The Dutch began a drainage project and reclaimed the flat land between the Pitt and Alouette rivers that was formerly known as Alouette (or Lillooet) Slough.

An island located about halfway up Pitt Lake was inhabited early last century. Named variously Wright Island, Goose Island or Pen Island, in 1906 it was the site of a prison camp that was later abandoned.

The island contained excellent quarry stone and timber that was used to build the B.C. Penitentiary. The following is an excerpt from a report dated August 28, 1906, by the warden, Mr. M.C. Whyte:

> We have opened up Wright Island quarry, Pitt Lake, situated 27 miles from here by water. We have there 15 convicts under a trade inspector, and expect before the season closes, about the first of September, to have about 200 cords of wood, and 500 tons of rock for foundations. Next season we hope to do better as it has taken about 6 weeks to erect log houses, wharf, etc.
>
> This quarry will only be worked about 3 months a year, and will supply a long felt want in wood for brick kiln and rock for foundations of new buildings.

Today, civilization has pushed farther up the lake. Logging operations are carried on at the head of the lake, and there is a fish hatchery at Alvin—near where Corbold Creek meets Pitt River.

Appendix C: A Word about Provenance

In the world of research, provenance is very important. Provenance speaks to the origin of something, to the ability to trace an artifact, a photograph, a letter, a report or any item of historical interest back to its creation, to confirm it is real. Thus, researchers make every attempt to trace things back to their origins.

Much of the Slumach story lacks any provenance whatsoever. Did a man named Slumach actually live? Certainly. While no birth records exist, newspaper accounts of his crime—and punishment—and the trial judge's bench book provide confirmation of that.

Did Jackson exist? Stories about him have, for over a century. But no actual record of his life exists, and deposit information from his San Francisco bank apparently—and inconveniently—disappeared in that city's 1906 earthquake. Thus, Jackson and his famous letter could be constructs, convenient creations thrown into the mix by someone to nudge along an early legend for their own benefit.

Did Molly Tynan exist? Perhaps. But we know Slumach was *not* hanged for *her* murder, thus the picture of her printed in many publications over the years has no provenance. How did it come into the legend? No one knows. It could be the picture of an early New Westminster resident named Molly Tynan, or it could simply be an old picture with no relation to the story, slipped in by an enthusiastic early newspaper editor to "round out" the copy.

The lack of provenance takes nothing away from the Slumach legend, for that is precisely why a legend is a legend! No one can prove whether or not it is true, thus it is based in speculation, rumour and exaggeration. But keeping the discussion alive promotes more research, and the possibility of provenance appearing just around the corner. We can only hope that this latest updating of the Slumach legend encourages others to continue the search for provenance in all the intriguing elements of this story.

Words of Appreciation

In 1972, we wrote these words of thanks:

> At the end of every book, words of thanks are given to all of those who assisted the author or authors in the preparation and publication of the work. The same trite phrases are written, and they always say something like "To all the people who helped me when I needed it most, who are too numerous to mention, who are ... etc."
>
> Now, having completed this book, we find ourselves needing to use the same phrases.
>
> This book is really many people. It is the people who supported us in our hopes of publishing a study of Slumach and his legendary mine. It is the people who called us to say "I have something you might be interested in ... " It is the people who helped out by making necessary trips here and there when the authors couldn't. It is the people who willingly shared their knowledge, advice and experience to make this whole thing possible. And it is the people who stood patiently by and allowed us to pursue our research at the risk of neglecting other important duties.
>
> And we thank them very sincerely for all their help.

Those words from 1972 have stood the test of time. Many ventures and more than three decades later, many other people have also earned our sincere appreciation. The authors thank all of the individuals who willingly shared their knowledge, advice, experience and material to help us create this 35th-anniversary edition of our quest for the truth behind Slumach's gold. We are especially grateful to Don Waite and Fred Braches, who made significant contributions by providing interesting input and angles that added to our book's thoroughness and credibility. We thank them for their generous assistance.

Rick Antonson, Mary Trainer
and Brian Antonson

Sources

In our 1972 edition we thanked the following sources: *The Columbian, The Native Voice, The RCMP Quarterly, B.C. Digest, Canada West, Enterprise, Canada Geological Survey,* the *Daily Colonist,* the *Vancouver Sun, Shoulder Strap,* the *Vancouver Province,* the British Columbia Provincial Archives, the New Westminster Library, the Vancouver Public Library, and Wayne Lyons, Frebo Studio and R. Harding, who helped to supply photos:

Books

Antonson, Brian. "Slumach's Glorious Gold," in *Canadian Frontier Annual.* Surrey, BC: Nunaga Publishing, 1976.

Friesen, Daryl. *Seekers of Gold.* Self-published e-book: www.bc-alter.net/dfriesen/mineintro.html. Accessed February 2007. Langley, BC: 2001.

Hawkins, Elizabeth. *Jack Mould and the Curse of Gold: Slumach's Legend Lives On.* Vancouver, BC: Hancock House Publishers Ltd., 1993.

Historical Society of Pitt Meadows. *Pitt Meadows Through a Century of Progress as Told In Part by Mary A. Park to Edith M. McDermottt.* Canadian Confederation Centennial Committee of Pitt Meadows, 1967.

Nicholson, R.W. *Lost Creek Mine.* Self-published e-book: www.rhistory4u.com/pittlakelegend.htm. Accessed February 2007. Penticton, BC: 2003.

Ramsey, Edgar. *Slumach: The Lost Mine.* Sonora, California: Ramsey Books, 2006.

Paterson, T.W. "Legend of the Lost Creek Mine," in *Lost Bonanzas of Western Canada,* Garnet Basque, ed. Surrey: Heritage House Publishing, 1999, reprinted 2006. Originally published in *Canadian Treasure Trails.* Langley, BC: Stagecoach Publishing, 1976.

Waite, Donald E. *Kwant'stan.* Self-published: Maple Ridge, 1972.

Waite, Donald E. *The Fraser Valley Story.* Hancock House Publishers Ltd., 1988.

Telephone interviews

Michael Collier, interviewed by Rick Antonson March 21, 2007.
Jon Ferry, interviewed by Brian Antonson January 16, 2007.
John Lovelace, interviewed by Rick Antonson March 20, 2007.
Rob Nicholson, interviewed by Brian Antonson January 16, 2007.

Personal interviews

Fred Braches, interviewed by Rick Antonson February 3, 2007.

Daryl Friesen, interviewed by Mary Trainer February 19, 2007.
Don Waite, interviewed by Rick Antonson February 3, 2007.

Magazines and newspaper articles

Antonson, Rick A. "Slumach's Curse." *Beautiful B.C.*, Spring 1972,
pp. 1–16.

Barlee, N.L. "The Lost Mine of Pitt Lake," *Canada West*, Winter 1970,
pp. 10–15.

Ferry, Jon. "Gold Fever! Looking for the Lost Creek Mine." *The Province*,
October 9, 11, 12, 13 and 14, 1983.

Hume, Mark. "Alberta couple survive 'curse' tracking legendary gold
mine." The *Vancouver Sun*, October 10, 1995.

Television programs

Treasure Hunters: The Mystery of Old Slumach, episode 10. Germany:
Tandem Films, 1991.

Curse of the Lost Gold Mine. Vancouver: Yaletown Productions Inc., 1994.

Wings Over Canada, Episode 507. Vancouver: ATV Productions, 2005.

Exhibit Eh! Exposing Canada, One Mystery at a Time. "The Sinister Plots,"
episode 10: Delta: Big Red Barn Productions, 2007.

Other websites

www.slumach.ca
www.yaletownentertainment.com
www.wingsovercanada.ca

Photos

Daily Columbian: pp. 40, 139, 160 (left)
Daryl Friesen: p. 11
Don Waite: pp. 12, 34, 52, 53, 64, 67, 69, 72, 102, 106, 135
Fred Bosman: sketches pp. 49, 51, 59, 125, 128
Heritage House collection: pp. 16, 20, 36, 38, 42, 45, 94, 103, 115, 125
(right top and bottom)
Michael Collier: pp. 62, 74, 84, 86, 88, 89, 92, 119, 120 and 121 (bottom),
122, 125 (top left)
Neil Trainer: p. 160 (right)
Rob Nicholson: pp. 112, 114, 118, 121 (top)
Roy McMartyn (provided by Harry Corder): pp. 56, 57
Tourism British Columbia: pp. 9, 13, 76, 78, 81, 97, 98, 109, 137, 140, 144

Index

Authors Mary Trainer, Rick Antonson and Brian Antonson (left to right) work on their original book in 1971 and on this one in 2007.

BRIAN ANTONSON, RICK ANTONSON and MARY TRAINER, all born and raised in British Columbia, were in their early 20s when they collaborated to write and publish *In Search of a Legend: Slumach's Gold* in 1972. The incentive to create the book actually originated two years earlier as a way to celebrate the centennial of B.C.'s entry into Confederation in 1971. Inspired by the afterglow of Canada's centennial and Expo 67, the trio was part of a new generation that was passionate about being Canadian—and about all things Canadian, especially our history, our outdoors, and local authors who had incredible stories to share about our beloved province. Rick, Mary and Brian created their own house, Nunaga (the Inuit word for "my land, my country") Publishing, and between 1972 and 1979 they published more than 25 books under this imprint and Antonson Publishing.

Since then, they have achieved successful careers in broadcast education, tourism and communications in Metro Vancouver—but still dream about a long-lost mine waiting to be discovered—somewhere out there in the wilderness near Pitt Lake.

Readers can contact the authors at slumachsgold@yahoo.ca.